FabJob Guide to

Become a Home Stager

KIMBERLY M. STONE

FABJOB® GUIDE TO BECOME A HOME STAGER

by Kimberly M. Stone

ISBN: 978-1-897286-06-7

Library and Archives Canada Cataloguing in Publication

Stone, Kimberly M., 1976-
FabJob guide to become a home stager or redesigner /
by Kimberly M. Stone.

Accompanied by a CD.
Includes bibliographical references.
ISBN 978-1-897286-06-7

1. House selling. 2. Interior decoration--Vocational guidance.
3. Real estate business--Vocational guidance.
I. Title. II. Title: Become a home stager or redesigner.

HD1379.S788 2007 333.33'8068 C2007-901541-7

About the Websites Mentioned in this Guide: Although we aim to provide the information you need within the guide, we have also included a number of websites because readers have told us they appreciate knowing about sources of additional information. (**TIP:** Don't include a period at the end of a web address when you type it into your browser.) Due to the constant development of the Internet, websites can change. Any websites mentioned in this guide are included for the convenience of readers only. We are not responsible for the content of any sites except FabJob.com.

FabJob Inc.
19 Horizon View Court
Calgary, Alberta, Canada T3Z 3M5

FabJob Inc.
4616 25th Avenue NE, #224
Seattle, Washington, USA 98105

To order books in bulk, phone 403-949-2039
To arrange a media interview, phone 403-949-4980

www.FabJob.com
THE DREAM CAREER EXPERTS

Contents

About the Authors

As a lifelong Texas resident, lead author **Kimberly M. Stone** has seen success in both the business world and in the exhilarating field of interior decorating.

Kimberly attended the University of Texas at Arlington where she fulfilled a Bachelor of Business Administration degree with a concentration in Marketing. She then worked for six years in marketing and advertising with several well-known product and service corporations. This valuable experience allowed Kimberly to make use of her natural design talent through retail merchandising, trade show exhibits, product displays, and photo shoot styling.

Even though she has been decorating as a sideline for a number of years, Kimberly officially launched herself as an independent interior decorator in 2003. Her specialized training includes the completion of the Advanced Home Interior Design Program at Tarrant County College in Fort Worth, Texas, along with an internship at an upscale design studio.

Her passion for decorating and a desire to educate others about the industry led Kimberly to pursue freelance writing on the subject. She is currently a staff writer for MySpaceDesigners.com and LoveToKnow.com's Interior Design site, as well as completing numerous other design-related writing projects.

Kimberly is the owner of Adore Your Décor™, an interior decorating firm specializing in interior redesigns and home staging, as well as offering full-service interior decorating.

Visit her website at **www.adoreyourdecor.com.**

Contributing author **Moona Masri-Whitice** (IRIS) graduated from the University of Miami with a degree in Communications and originally worked in the travel industry specializing in Marketing and Training. Since 2001, following in the footsteps of her father, an architect in Broward County, Florida, she has dedicated herself to the art of redesign and interior decorating. She owns her own business, Perfectlyou Décor, and is an interior redesign specialist-stager, an interior decorator, and a Dewey Color Consultant. She believes in "redefining spaces that redesign lives." She teaches interior decorating courses at Broward Community College in Florida as an Adjunct Professor and is a proud member of the Dewey Color System Advisory Committee.

Contributing author **Nancy Cook-Geoghegan** (IRIS; IDS; NAPO) is president of One Day Décor, a company specializing in interior décor, redesign and staging. Nancy is also president of Redesign America Interior Redesign School which offers training in Redesign and Staging, and is Co-Chair of the IRIS Training Committee. A published author, she has written for the Home and Garden section of the Fort Lauderdale Sun-Sentinel, contributed to a syndicated column in major newspapers throughout the U.S., and is a contributor to *IRIS in the House,* award-winner in the "Home: Decorating/Interior Design" category of the Best Books 2006 Book Awards and award-winning finalist in the "Anthologies: Non-Fiction" category of the Best Books 2006 Book Awards. She and her companies have been featured on NBC TV. Visit her website at **www.onedaydecor.com**.

Acknowledgements

Thank you to the following experts (listed alphabetically) for generously sharing home staging insider information, and business and marketing advice in this FabJob guide. Opinions in this guide are those of the author or editors and not necessarily those of experts interviewed for this guide.

- *Lauren Bartel*
  Interior Redesign and Home Staging Professional
  www.newdawndecor.com

- *Toni Pruett Bouman*
  Toni B Interiors
  www.ToniBouman.com

- *Nancy J. Busse*
  Writer, editor, and public relations consultant

- *Cheryl Clifford, IADA, RES*
  A NEW VIEW - Interior Enhancement by Cheryl
  www.interiorenhancement.com

- *Gillian Cunningham*
  Real Estate Consultant/Broker, ASP, ABR, e-Pro, GRI
  Prestique Realty
  www.PrestiqueRealty.com

- *Julie Dana*
  The Home Stylist
  Author, *The Complete Idiot's Guide to Staging Your Home to Sell*
  East Aurora, NY
  www.thehomestylist.com

- *Sandy Dixon*
  Interior Arrangements, Inc.
  www.interiorarrangements.com

- *Diana Ezerins*
  Real Estate Enhancement Specialist
  Diana Ezerins Interiors
  www.DianaEzerins.com

- *Susan Fruit*
  Susan Fruit Interiors
  www.SusanFruitInteriors.com

- *Ilyce R. Glink*
  Real Estate and Financial Expert
  www.thinkglink.com

- *Debra Gould, The Staging Diva®*
  President, Six Elements Inc.
  www.stagingdiva.com
  www.sixelements.com

- *Joanne B. Hans, Owner*
  A Perfect Placement
  www.aperfectplacement.com

- *Millie Harris-Hayes*
  Interior Designer
  Illusion Designs

- *Kim Kapellusch*
  Prepared to Sell
  Valencia, CA
  www.preparedtosellstaging.com

- *JoAnne Lenart-Weary*
  One Day Decorating
  www.onedaydecorating.com
  www.oddaa.com

- *Lori Matzke, President*
  Center Stage Home, Inc.
  www.centerstagehome.com
- *Jason Maxwell, ASP*
  President of IAHSP,
  Dallas Chapter
  Equity Enhancers Home Staging
  www.eestaging.com
- *Annie Pinsker-Brown*
  Stage to Sell
  Los Angeles, CA
  www.StageToSell.biz
- *Robin Rosen*
  President, Stageffect, Inc.
  Chappaqua, New York
  www.stageffect.com
- *Darla Rowley*
  IMPACT! Interior Design
  Solutions
  Royal Oak, MI
  www.impactids.com
- *Charlene Storozuk*
  Home Design Consultant,
  Dezigner DigzTM
  Regional Vice-President, Canada,
  Real Estate Staging Association
  Burlington, Ontario
  www.dezignerdigz.com
- *Val Sharp, Owner*
  Sharp ReDesigns
  President, Canadian Redesigners
  Association
  www.sharpredesigns.com

We would also like to thank Steve Clemons (**www.steveclemonsphotography.com**) and Peter Krupenye of Peter Krupenye Photography for photos used in the color section of this guide.

1. Introduction

Welcome to your fabulous future as a home stager! According to *Entrepreneur* magazine, home staging is a "hot" business, so you've picked a perfect career for success. The demand for home stagers is growing steadily as more and more homeowners learn about the service and its benefits. You can be ready for this surge of continued interest in home staging by entering the field now.

You may have seen home staging on TV or read about it in a magazine, inspiring you to investigate how to enter this exciting field and leading you to this guide. During your research, you probably came across training programs that last only a few days but cost a few thousand dollars. However, many up-and-coming entrepreneurs cannot afford pricey programs like these when first starting out, nor can they wait around for the next scheduled training session. If you want to get your home staging business off the ground now with little money up front, the *FabJob Guide to Become a Home Stager* will give you the information you need to get started, and much more.

1.1 A Career in Home Staging

1.1.1 Why Choose Home Staging?

From first-hand experience, I've discovered that working for yourself and building a business are far more rewarding than working for someone else ever will be. Not only on an emotional level, but also because your earning potential is not dependent on fiscal budgets or biased employee evaluations. Being the boss, you control your work schedule, how much your business grows, and how much income you make.

How many homes are listed for sale in your neighborhood right now? What about city-wide? Don't forget about the condos, apartments, and commercial properties. Chances are good that hundreds of homes and properties are listed for sale in your area, and many more are entering the market daily. All of these properties need to be staged before entering the competitive real estate marketplace.

Luckily, many homeowners and real estate agents have heard of staging and know how fundamental it is for moving a property faster and for more money. This is where you come in. As a home stager, you will work in beautiful homes and be paid quite nicely for it as well. You will work directly with homeowners or in conjunction with top real estate agents. And, because of the proven marketing techniques you will learn later in this guide, they will know about your service and know how to contact you.

Jason Maxwell of Equity Enhancers wholeheartedly believes that "home staging is about changing lives...one house, family, and real estate market at a time! If you are looking to help change the way America sells homes, then home staging is the business for you." This FabJob guide will provide you with all the insider information needed to launch yourself as a successful home stager.

1.1.2 What is Home Staging?

Home Staging vs. Interior Redesign or Interior Decorating

Home staging differs in a number of ways from interior redesigning and interior decorating. First, the primary task of a home stager is to help homeowners and realtors sell houses. This focus makes a home stager's tasks fairly specific and different from both interior redesigning and interior decorating, even though they do overlap to some degree.

For example, an interior decorator helps people to redecorate interior spaces. This might involve redecorating a single room or an entire house. The decorator might help a client to choose new furniture, create an entirely new decorating theme, replace window and wall coverings, add color or create an entirely new color scheme, replace flooring, and so on. Interior decorators are hired not just for homes, but to redecorate offices, restaurants, and any other spaces where decorating makes an impression on the people who use or visit the space.

An interior redesigner is essentially an interior decorator working without the big budget. Interior redesigners help clients to redecorate their living or working spaces using furniture and accessories they already have. Like interior decorating, interior redesign might also include coming up with a new color scheme, repainting walls, adding more accessories, and removing furniture and accessories that don't fit in.

Now, compare this to tasks typical of home staging. In a nutshell, home staging is the process of making a house buyer-friendly. The public at large assumes they can envision a space without bias, despite being presented with garish decorating choices or stark, empty rooms. In reality, they often have a hard time seeing a home's potential, no matter how good their imaginations may be. Homebuilders don't market new homes by showing an empty or cluttered model—they tastefully make each model home as enticing as possible to buyers. This is because a buyer must be able to immediately picture living in the home before they ever buy it.

The main ingredients in home staging include:

- Highlighting a home's best features
- Certifying a home's cleanliness
- Abolishing the clutter in a home
- Neutralizing the color palette of a home
- Seeing a home from the buyer's perspective
- Depersonalizing a home

Some in the industry use the term "real estate enhancement" as an alternate name for staging. This seems especially appropriate because that's exactly what home staging can do. It enhances the best features of a property while improving or downplaying the not-so-great features along the way.

With staging, any potential problems with a home's cosmetic appearance or basic functions can be addressed early in the selling process. Staging can prevent a house from sitting on the market too long and prevent a seller from lowering their asking price.

1.1.3 Typical Tasks of Home Stagers

Along with using your creativity to stage homes, you will also need some resourcefulness and organizational skills in order to tackle numerous tasks essential to managing your business. We'll look at the specific skills and knowledge you will need later on in this guide. On an average day, you may be involved to some degree with any or all of the following activities:

- Marketing and advertising your business, including website creation and updates.
- Returning calls to potential and existing clients.
- Making appointments with new clients and managing your daily schedule.

- Calling on clients in their homes for consultations.
- Drafting proposals or bids for your services.
- Presenting and selling proposals to clients.
- Writing up contracts or letters of agreement for your services.
- Staging homes.
- Managing work crews or assistants.
- Sourcing, ordering, and keeping inventory of all necessary supplies and staging props and materials.
- Collecting deposits, balances, and any unpaid amounts from clients.
- Keeping good business records, paying state and federal taxes, and maintaining business licenses.
- Establishing alliances with reputable service providers to use as subcontractors or to recommend to your clients.

1.1.4 Services Provided by a Home Stager

In the field of home staging, there is room for a variety of service offerings. Many homeowners have busy lives, and they need the help and knowledge of a professional in order to get a project completed quickly. However, some people are "do-it-yourselfers" who will want to carry out your recommendations on their own.

Here are some typical home stager service offerings:

Assessing Interior Spaces

The first step in any successful home staging project is assessing the space. Here you will do a walk-through with your client, inspecting the home room by room, checking for deficiencies, looking for ways to improve what you see and making notes. This service can either be a stand-alone service or incorporated into an overall home staging project.

Consulting

As a home staging consultant you will meet with clients to discuss their home staging needs. Rather than carrying out any work for the client, you will merely provide them with an analysis of their interior and exterior spaces. You will give them recommendations for how to stage the home, either on the spot, or in a detailed report delivered or sent electronically later.

Staging

This involves assessing the home and performing some or all of the tasks mentioned in section 1.1.2. The typical home staging project entails everything from removing over-sized furniture to decluttering to getting rid of unpleasant odors. Sometimes, you will be assisted in these tasks by the homeowners themselves, and other times you will be left on your own to complete the project without the involvement of the homeowner. You may or may not be working with subcontractors.

Additional Services

One way to increase your earning potential is to expand your service offerings and catch the attention of a wider customer base.

Home Organizing

Home organizational services would be a natural fit, because part of home staging is clearing the clutter in a home. You can help clients organize closets, cabinets, and entire rooms by working hands-on or suggesting products to optimize their organization.

Personal Shopping

Another practical service to add would be personal shopping. You will save your clients valuable time by doing the legwork for them. If a client has authorized you to purchase items, make sure there is a return policy or you'll be stuck with a piece if the client doesn't choose it from the presented options.

Interior Redesign

Many home stagers offer interior redesign services to clients. Interior redesign is similar to interior decorating, but there is less emphasis on adding brand new elements to the rooms (such as new furniture, window treatments, flooring, etc.). Rather, you will work with what the client already has and create a more organized whole. Like home staging, interior redesign often begins with a process of cleaning, decluttering and organizing.

Full Service Interior Decorating

Full-service interior decorating is another lucrative way to expand your business. This involves helping clients with an extensive assortment of items including: furniture, wall coverings, window treatments, bedding, upholstery, paint, flooring, rugs, lighting, and complete remodeling projects. As you can see, full-service interior decorating requires getting acquainted with numerous products and establishing contacts with a variety of specialty contractors.

1.2 Adding Value in Today's Real Estate Market

You may be thinking, "These are tough times, people are losing their homes, the real estate market has collapsed across North America; how will I ever find work in this kind of market?" Rest assured that even, or especially, in difficult economic times home stagers are a much needed resource for realtors and homeowners.

A poll conducted recently by Royal LePage Real Estate Services (**www.royallepage.ca/CMSTemplates/GlobalNavTemplate.aspx?id=1045**), highlights the fact that first impressions are everything in the real estate market. Actually, most potential buyers make up their minds about a house within the first few minutes of viewing it. The poll also found that while a majority of home buyers said they preferred to view a home without furnishings, an unstaged home lacking furniture and other décor tends to allow buyers to focus on the negative details.

According to Dianne Usher, senior manager, Royal LePage Real Estate Services, "A contemporary and minimalist space with neutral coloured walls and a limited number of personal items appeals to most buyers and ensures the best results when selling a home." Creating this kind of space is exactly what a home stager does.

According to a May 2004 article in MoneySense magazine, home stagers have been proven to help sell homes quicker and for more money. The article reports that in a survey of nearly 3,000 properties in eight major U.S. cities by Coldwell Banker Realty, the average home sold in about a month, while staged homes typically sold in about two weeks. In addition, staged homes sold for 4.7% more on average than non-staged homes.

Of course, today's real estate market is not what it was even just a few years ago. Still, homeowners and realtors continue to seek out home stagers to help them make their homes stand out in a buyers' market. Staging a home depersonalizes it and helps buyers to imagine themselves living there, making it easier to sell by helping it show better and look its best in marketing photos. Both homeowners and realtors are also more aware of home staging thanks to television shows on networks like HGTV and are more likely to consider home staging as a way to help them sell a house.

Staging a home has other value, too. Consider that in order to sell their homes, many homeowners often must make the difficult decision to drop their price in order to sell their property. Given that staging a home has been proven to sell homes faster and for more money, making an investment of a few hundred dollars to stage their home can save homeowners thousands of dollars over dropping the price of the house.

Another related aspect is that, in selling homes in a buyers' market, there is often more of a need for a homeowner to be willing to negotiate their asking price. If they already have a "rock bottom" price they are willing to accept, you can help them to stay above that price by making their home more enticing to prospective buyers. Obviously, there is great potential for a home stager's skills and talents even in a difficult real estate market.

In addition to maximizing home selling prices in a tough real estate market, home staging also has a positive effect on a neighborhood or community as a whole. When a house sells, it influences the market value of surrounding homes. If the selling price is higher at a staged house than it would have been otherwise, the value of the homes in that area can be affected positively. Staging can create stronger real estate markets one property at a time.

1.3 Benefits of Being a Home Stager

Working in this industry has so many rewarding benefits, especially for those with a knack for decorating or the need for a flexible career. Aside from the customizable work schedule and unlimited income potential, it's such a joy to use your creativity on a daily basis. This work can also be heartwarming as you help clients tap into life-changing equity on the sale of their home.

Work from Home

Home staging is a career tailor-made for a home office. The primary reason is that the bulk of your work will take place in your clients' homes. Being less than sixty seconds away from your kitchen and bedroom can be one of the many benefits of working from home.

Obviously, this can also be very distracting as you try to write your proposals and handle an assortment of business details. You will need to be a self-motivator in order to stay focused. The best way to do this is to set aside a designated office space for your business. A spare bedroom or study will work great, but you can also use part of your living room, garage, or other free area separated by a room divider or tall folding screen.

Express Your Creativity

There are very few things in life as exciting and stimulating as generating imaginative ideas and putting them into practical use. This line of work provides endless opportunities to exercise your creativity and problem solving skills while getting paid for it in the process. Not only will you be finding resourceful uses for a homeowner's furniture and accessories, you will also consult with them on color palettes, fabric choices, and much more.

Real estate enhancement specialist Diana Ezerins feels that "it is imperative to stay current on both real estate market trends and interior design trends because you straddle both industries." When you actively gather new knowledge and inspiration, you'll have more creative ideas to show your clients.

Help People Who Need It

Expediting the sale of a client's property by staging to its full potential is a good deed in many ways. The most tangible way to see this is when a client receives more money than originally expected for their property. This extra money can be used to purchase a new home, pay off debt, send their kids to college, or help them to care for an elderly parent.

Staging can also help people's lives in other ways. For example, a person who has recently lost a spouse may need to move to a smaller residence or apartment in order to make ends meet. They will be grateful for a quick sale and any extra equity that can be made along the way.

As well, it can be stressful when a family is temporarily split up because their current home hasn't sold yet, and mom or dad must begin a new job in a different town. A decision must be made as to who will stay and get the house sold, so the quicker it can sell the better.

You Can Start Right Now

With low start-up costs, becoming a home stager is something you can start as soon as you finish reading this guide. The typical base amount needed to launch a home staging business is about $500 to $1,000. However, you can spend more or less than this, depending on what equipment and supplies you currently have on hand.

As with any new venture, it is smart to start small and test the waters. You may be able to do this while still employed by someone else and then transition to running your business full-time as your client base and revenues grow. Saving up three to six months worth of living expenses will help this switch go more smoothly and may keep you from needing a small business loan, but isn't absolutely necessary.

TIP: There's not really a need for an elaborate office when you're first starting out. You should earmark most of your start-up money for marketing and promoting your new business.

1.4 Inside This Guide

The *FabJob Guide to Become a Home Stager* will take you step-by-step through everything you'll need to start out and succeed in your new career. Each chapter is full of important information, helpful advice, and useful tips from experts in this exciting and rewarding field.

In Chapter 2, we'll take you through the specialty service areas you might want to consider before starting your home staging business. Then you'll discover how to meet with clients and assess their home staging needs. We'll also show you how to assess the spaces you will transform for them and become their chosen home stager. After reading about the tools and equipment you'll need, you will learn "How to Stage a Home" using the design elements and principles you'll read about in this chapter. You'll find out how to organize and "declutter" the home, as well as how to hide blemishes before bringing it all together by arranging and decorating the space using a variety of props, artwork, furniture and accessories. Finally, in this chapter, we'll tell you how to find, hire and work with contractors you may need to fulfill your vision of your client's fully staged home.

Chapter 3 will help you to get ready. What skills and knowledge will you need? Where can you learn more about home staging? What training programs are available? What professional associations can you join to help you as you get started? How can you find jobs in related fields to prepare you for your new career? The answers to these questions and more are in this chapter.

Chapter 4 explains the business aspects of starting your own home staging company. We'll show you how to create a business plan, find financing and name your company. You'll also learn about home staging franchises that are available to you. We'll help you answer the following questions: What start-up expenses can I expect? Where can I get financing if I need it? What are some of the legal aspects I should consider? We'll also help you learn more about working with support staff and how to hire the help you need.

Learn about "Getting Clients" in Chapter 5. You will learn various strategies for marketing your business such as how to create your own website, types of advertising you can use and where to advertise, and how to get free publicity for your company. Discover the potential of networking with other business professionals and where to find others who can help your business to prosper.

Finally, in Chapter 6, you will read the stories of some people just like you who started out in the home staging industry and went on to create very successful businesses.

When you have finished reading this guide, you will understand the skills and knowledge you will need to succeed and where to go to find additional help and resources. By following the advice and using the valuable resources included you will be on your way to success as a home stager. Let's get started!

2. What a Home Stager Does

In the first section of this chapter, we'll look at some basic home staging service specialties to give you ideas about the kind of home staging business you can start. Once you've decided on your specialty and set up your business (as described in upcoming chapters), you'll be ready to start working with clients.

In this chapter, we'll also show you how to conduct a client consultation. This process includes meeting with your clients, assessing their needs, then going through their home and assessing the space within it from a home stager's perspective. Once you've completed this, and you think you're willing to work with the client, we'll show you how to present a proposal for your services and get them to sign a contract for your services. Contracts are important in this business, because they outline exactly what work you will do and how much you will be paid for it.

This chapter will also take you through the entire process of staging a home. First, we'll take a look at the equipment and supplies you will need. Then, once you're equipped, you'll have a lot of work to do. In section 2.4 you'll get an overview of the entire process room by room.

Subsequent sections then provide details on each of the tasks involved in home staging.

Your first task will be to organize and get rid of the clutter around the house. This is how you begin depersonalizing the home. We'll look at how to make a home look as attractive as possible by decluttering and cleaning throughout the entire house, plus how to mask damage that's too costly to repair. Next the guide explains how to decorate the rooms to enhance the home's best features. You'll learn about creating an overall design theme for the home, and how to work with the various elements of a room including the walls, windows, flooring, furniture, and accessories.

You'll also find special tips for staging a vacant home, learn how to create "curb appeal" to make a home's exterior look attractive, and get advice on how to create "ambience" to help buyers immediately feel good about the home.

Finally, we'll tell you about working with different types of contractors. These are important adjuncts to your home staging business, as they will be the ones who do all the non-design related work like making complex repairs. We'll show you how to find and choose a good contractor and give you some advice for paying them for the work they do for you and your clients.

2.1 Home Staging Specialties

Although home staging is generally thought of as a niche service inside the world of interior decorating, you can specialize still further. One way to do this is to target your marketing efforts towards a particular group that you understand well and relate to on a personal level. For example, marketing to your ethnic community will yield very good results because the customer base will feel comfortable with you almost instantly. Here are some other ideas for identifying niche markets:

Demographic Groups

You can focus your marketing and advertising on any number of groups based on age, gender, ethnicity, or income bracket. If you have a connection to the senior citizen community, they would probably love to hear about your services. Many retirees sell their homes in order to downsize or so they can move to posh retirement communities.

Commercial and Retail

While most will be working in the residential sector, there are opportunities on the commercial side as well. If you have a corporate background or a similar group of contacts, try connecting with them for any decorating needs that may arise for special events or holidays. Maybe they've been thinking about making their lobby more inviting with new furniture and artwork.

Another commercial segment to look into is retail merchandising. Large furniture stores, boutiques, and design studios need space planning and staged vignettes to help sell their wares and draw in customers.

2.1.1 Full-Service Home Staging

A remarkable advantage in this line of work is the cornucopia of service offerings from which to choose. Since you can't be everything to everybody, you'll need to decide what services initially should be marketed to your clients. You should start with a focus in home staging and then see what other type of projects are most often requested.

The popularity of many services is dependent upon the market conditions and the demographics of the people in each region. If there are a lot of young families in your area, then organizational services will probably be perfect for busy families who have a great deal of bits and pieces cluttering their homes.

Being your own boss means that you'll have complete control over what services to provide. Consider your own background and personal interests when making the choice of what offerings will be the most beneficial.

You can choose almost any combination of these potential services:

- Home staging
- Open House detailing
- Move-in services

- Organizing
- Color consultation
- Shopping trips or personal shopping
- Full service interior decorating (custom window treatments, upholstery, floral arrangements, or decorative painting)
- Landscaping and garden design
- Other related services (feng shui, child-proofing, etc.)

Typical clients for home stagers include:

- Homeowners selling with or without the services of a realtor
- Realtors
- Home builders

Other potential clients include:

- Furniture stores
- Home décor stores
- Department stores selling furniture or home accessories

Homeowners often hire home stagers when they are selling their homes on their own without the assistance of a realtor. Providing consulting services for homeowners like these is fairly common, although you may also be asked to carry out a full staging project. Alternatively, homeowners might hire you based on a recommendation from the realtor they are working with to sell their homes. If you can find a realtor who really likes your work, you can become their preferred home stager to recommend to clients.

Realtors hire home stagers for a couple of reasons. Often, they provide a home staging service to sellers they're working with as a complimentary service. You may become the preferred stager for a particular real estate company and they might hire you exclusively on a contract basis to stage all their clients' homes. Realtors may also hire a home stager when they feel that the client's home is just not living up to its potential due to excessive clutter, odors, poorly coordinated décor, bad flow, and so on. In this case, you will probably be hired on an as-needed basis and paid either by the realtor or by the homeowner, depending on the agreement you reach with the parties concerned.

Home builders often hire home stagers to help them with coordinating and implementing a décor plan for one or more model homes. Your job will be to fully decorate, in a non-personal manner, the entire model home from living room to kitchen to bathrooms to bedrooms. They may also ask you to stage outdoor spaces like patios and decks, too. Becoming a preferred stager for a particular builder is also another desirable position to attain.

Home builders frequently work with various organizations to raffle homes for charity. Raffle homes are usually featured online in promotional materials, and they are open to people touring them. These homes, like model homes, need to be staged in order to entice people into purchasing tickets. Similarly, staged vignettes and furniture arrangements for retailers entices people to buy their products.

You'll learn more about how to perform full-service staging later in this chapter.

2.1.2 Home Staging Consulting Services

Instead of all the other home staging service offerings, you can choose to provide just consultations to your clients. If you need to work part-time in your business, this is one way to keep the workflow to a manageable level.

As a specialist home staging consultant, you will draft a plan of action that your homeowner can implement in order to maximize the sale of their home. This will involve room-by-room recommendations, as well as suggestions for their exterior spaces.

Assessment and Report Services

One consulting opportunity is to provide no more than just your recommendations to the client. This still means that you won't be carrying out the suggestions or staging a home yourself. Consultations like this are especially sought after by homeowners who have the capability and time to carry out your recommendations, but need some professional advice and a creative eye to get started.

Clients with limited budgets will also appreciate this type of affordable consulting service. They will get expert suggestions that they can then implement into a useable plan.

Contractor Referral Services

Another consulting area you can make extra money from is in referring your clients to recommended professional services related to your home staging business. These include housecleaning and maid services, handyman and repair services, carpet cleaners, professional organizers, landscapers, painters, and storage facilities, to name a few. You should make contact with other local businesses that offer services your clients will likely need.

Researching Contractors

Busy homeowners will likely go with your business referrals because it saves them the time and headache of tracking down fair-priced, dependable service contractors. It helps if you have confidence in the companies you are referring and if you truly believe they are the best at what they do.

Make sure that you carefully research each company, talk to other people about their reputation, and check with your local Better Business Bureau office to ensure that you are referring the best businesses to your clients. You could even test out their services in your own home first.

Because they were referred by you, a contractor's level of customer service will reflect on you. If a client has a problem with one of the businesses you referred, they might even call you hoping that you'll be an intermediary for them. Use caution in this area, but also try to keep your past clients satisfied so that they will keep referring your services by positive word of mouth advertising, the most valuable kind to have. To learn more about working with contractors, see section 2.11.

2.1.3 Other Specialties

Event and Party Staging

Event and party staging is another specialty for home stagers. You can offer this as a primary service specialty or simply as an extra to your regular service offerings.

Event and party staging entails providing props, such as table settings, flowers, and other decorations, setting the tables, and decorating the interior of the party venue. You will either work alone or with event and party planners as a subcontractor. You may also work with caterers, typically as a subcontractor.

Another, related category in this type of staging is holiday staging. This means staging a client's home or business for a single holiday event, including decorating and installing props that will be taken away after the event. For example, you could offer a Christmas staging service and provide a fully decorated tree, themed decorations and accessories both inside and outside the house, as well as lights, dishes, candles, etc. Your fee will include both the decorating service and prop rental.

Outdoor Staging

Outdoor staging, like event and party staging, is another specialty niche that may or may not include working for a client who is selling their home. This type of staging can also be performed in conjunction with a party or event.

Your clients for this service might include homeowners or realtors who feel that the outdoor living space (patio, deck, or yard) might not be living up to its full potential. Buyers want to be able to see themselves enjoying the outdoor living spaces along with the rest of the house. A cluttered backyard with worn exterior furnishings on the patio or deck, or with sagging fences or dead plants has little appeal to buyers.

Your job will be to make the outdoor space more appealing by installing props, cleaning up yard clutter, making sure all the plants are in good shape and so on. Props can include barbecues (outdoor grills, cooking and serving facilities, etc.), patio or lawn furniture, lighting, etc. You may or may not include landscaping suggestions or suggested repairs in the project and help to implement these corrections.

2.2 Staging Equipment and Supplies

Along with equipping your home-based office (see section 4.1.5), you'll need additional tools and supplies for your staging projects. You should evaluate how much you can buy at the beginning and think about where you will store these items as well.

Even though you probably will start off with very few staging items, you will eventually build up your own stash of furniture and props in order to increase your profit margins. It's best to continually add new items and keep your existing inventory in top condition, so that your home staging supplies will be fresh and attractive. Toni Bouman of Toni B Interiors, a home stager with over two decades of experience in real estate, says, "After every close of escrow, I take several hundred dollars and purchase artwork, linens, and small furniture items that can work in a variety of settings... so I add as I go."

If you're planning to equip your business immediately with a variety of props, you'll need to think about storage space, whether you choose your own garage or an offsite storage facility. You'll probably also need shelving, storage boxes, or plastic containers to keep your supplies organized. A hand truck will be very useful for moving large items or heavy boxes, and you may need one for rearranging bulky items on your jobs.

While you may work with a contractor who cleans your clients' houses, you should have your own supply of cleaning tools, just in case you need to step in and help. The basic cleaning items to stockpile include a vacuum cleaner, dusting rags, window cleaner, multi-surface cleaner, a broom, and a mop.

2.2.1 What You'll Need

To make your home staging more efficient, you will need to build up a stockpile of useable props and accessories. This is a collection of items which you can use in a pinch when your clients just don't have the right piece on hand. You can retrieve these items after a house is sold or leave them for the client if the items are inexpensive.

One free source of props for staging is the outdoors. A branch or a few flowers from a client's yard can dress up a mantle or serve as a centerpiece on a coffee table when placed in a pretty vase. You can also use items from the garden like a small wooden bench or a weathered clay pot.

It pays to shop around for quality accessories and props. You are looking for superior items that are well-priced or on clearance. You can even try garage sales and thrift stores for excellent finds. Make sure the items are versatile enough for almost any décor, or it will be a waste of money if they can't be used often.

What kind of props should you look for when shopping? Anything that will multitask for several decorative uses would be a smart choice. You may also want to invest in a few signature inventory pieces such as classical artwork, tasteful silk floral arrangements, or dramatic candlesticks. These significant accessories can be used to add some excitement to a vacant home or just the right touch to a client's bare mantle.

Here are more than a few versatile items that your client may have on hand or that you should consider adding to your prop collection:

Folding tables and chairs

The perfect solution for an empty breakfast nook, or as a substitute for bulky furniture to create a more spacious dining room. Add a tablecloth and chair slipcovers for a finished look.

Inflatable air mattresses

Use to quickly furnish any unoccupied bedrooms or guest rooms. Choose air mattresses that sit at standard bed height like those made by AeroBed. Twin, full, or queen size air beds can be found in the $100-$300 price range, and many of them come with a built-in pump (otherwise, buy an electric air pump as well).

Baskets

Use as decorative items or as catch-alls to reduce clutter such as toiletries in a bathroom. A big basket on a fireplace hearth or on top of an armoire instills a warm, homey look.

Towels

Can be used in assorted sizes and colors to revamp any bathroom. Have an assortment of sets to complement a variety of décors; adorn towel bars and racks in endless creative ways, or roll up and place on a shelf or in a basket.

Flat bed sheets

Can masquerade as tablecloths, window treatments, or slipcovers. Naturally, sheets also come in handy for making an elegant bed ensemble, even on an inflatable mattress.

Tablecloths

Useful for covering plain tables, making window swags, or standing in as a comfy throw on a chaise lounge.

Pillows

A necessary decorative item for living rooms and bedrooms. Use a tailored design without ruffles to make throw pillows and bed pillows fit in with more décor styles. A few decorative pillows on a sofa or guest bed make for a more inviting room.

High-quality silk plants

A good investment, especially ivy vines, simple floral arrangements, and trees. A room devoid of greenery or color can benefit from a touch of natural-looking foliage, but use in moderation so the room is not overpowered.

Lamps and up lights

Essential props in your arsenal. A room with poor lighting is not an appealing room, unless you are sleeping! Use table lamps and floor lamps for general or task lighting, and use up lights to expand a room's corners or to make dramatic shadows by shining through a plant's leaves.

Fabrics

Fashion a bolt or remnant of attractive fabric into dozens of items like table toppers, window treatments, tablecloths, bed coverlets, furniture slipcovers, throws, pillow shams, and more. The clearance rack at your local fabric store is a fabulous source for inexpensive staging fabrics.

Shower curtains

Craft into window treatments, table runners, or use as a shower curtain tie-back to soften a bathtub.

Trimmings

Use raffia, ribbon, or corded rope to embellish almost anything including towels, pillows, vases, and window treatments. These quick and easy decorative details can be picked up at your local fabric or craft store.

Books

Attractive hard-covered books add a distinguished feel to a room. Fill in an empty bookcase or stack up as a base for plants and candle sticks.

Throws, blankets, and tapestries

Use anywhere there's a need for attractive or comfortable fabric.

Table settings

Breakfast tables or dining room tables look more welcoming to homebuyers than bare table tops. A few coordinated sets of plates, chargers, glasses, place mats, napkins, and napkin rings are the basic components. A breakfast nook might only need a couple of place settings laid out, while a dining room will look good with two to four place settings.

Artwork, mirrors, and wall décor

Key components to finishing out a space. You can find good-sized pieces that are both striking and tasteful for under $100.

Rugs

Rugs are a great foundation for furniture groupings when a room needs a little grounding or to add interest to a nondescript kitchen floor.

Choose area rugs with traditional and simple contemporary patterns, so they will fit with the majority of décors. You can keep a clean-edged look by opting against messy fringe. However, use some restraint with rugs to keep a staged home from feeling cluttered.

TIP: Keep a written list of any props or furniture used in staging each client's home so that you remember to retrieve all the pieces when the house sells. It may seem like you will remember each and every little item, but when you have several staged houses on the market and several more in progress it's easy to lose track of your inventory.

Tools of the Trade Checklist

Here's a handy checklist of necessary items for the home stager:

- ❑ Chalk line
- ❑ Clear fishing line
- ❑ Color wheel
- ❑ Cordless drill
- ❑ Cup hooks
- ❑ Dusting rags (or Swiffer dusters)
- ❑ Extension cords
- ❑ Furniture cleaner and polish
- ❑ Furniture sliders and lifter
- ❑ Furniture stain pens
- ❑ Glue
- ❑ Hammer
- ❑ Handheld steamer
- ❑ Handheld vacuum cleaner
- ❑ Kitchen gloves
- ❑ Level (small pocket size)

- ❑ Light bulbs
- ❑ Markers or Sharpies
- ❑ Marking pencils
- ❑ Nails (assorted sizes)
- ❑ Paint brushes
- ❑ Paint color fan
- ❑ Paper towels
- ❑ Picture hooks (box set for all weights)
- ❑ Picture wire kit
- ❑ Pliers
- ❑ Props
- ❑ Scissors
- ❑ Screwdriver (regular and flat head)
- ❑ Screws (assorted sizes)
- ❑ Sewing kit
- ❑ Spackle
- ❑ Spackle or putty knife
- ❑ Staple gun
- ❑ Step ladder
- ❑ Stud finder
- ❑ Tape measure
- ❑ Tapes (masking, duct, clear packing)
- ❑ Timers (for lamps or radios)
- ❑ Trash bags
- ❑ Trimmings (ribbon, raffia, rope)
- ❑ Utility knife
- ❑ Window cleaner

When your schedule becomes more demanding, you'll want a written inventory of all the furniture and props that were left at each jobsite. I suggest a simple log sheet that you and the homeowner both sign and date. Then, retrieving your inventory will be quick and hassle-free.

2.2.2 Where to Get Props and Furniture

Finding inexpensive and nice-looking accessories will presumably be easier than locating good deals on larger furniture pieces like sofas, chairs, beds, and tables. While you'll want to check out national furniture rental chains like Rent-A-Center (**www.rentacenter.com**) and Aaron Rents (**www.aaronrents.com**), start by researching the rates of all available local resources.

Look in the Yellow Pages under Furniture Renting and Leasing for national and local stores that rent furnishings. It is a good idea to contact as many of these retailers as you can, in order to figure out the going rental rates available to stagers in your area. You can then either pass on the rental costs to your clients, plus your markup, or refer your clients to the rental company of your choice.

When evaluating the various furniture rental companies, ask if they offer a commission program or decorator discount for sales that come through you. If the rental company does have a program, it could be structured in several different ways. For the most part, they do not discount their retail rental rates for stagers. Also, there may be additional fees that your client will need to pay. As an example, CORT Furniture, **www.cort.com/furniture/home-staging**, charges a 12% damage waiver fee and round-trip delivery and pickup cost of $115 (charges that you will need to pass on to your client). There can also be minimum rental amounts such as $500 per month for a two month lease or $350 per month for a three month lease.

A common plan involves bringing in or referring clients to their company which later sends you a percentage of that client's sales as a referral fee, such as 5% or 15%. Another possibility is that you place orders directly with the rental company and receive a decorator discount or commission rate. You might even consider networking with other local home stagers to share leased items or save on fees by combining your rental volume.

Of course, you may want to start your own personal inventory of props and furniture that you can then rent out to your clients. Lauren Bartel of New Dawn Décor says, "There are a few sources in my area that rent by the week or month. I also find inexpensive accessories and linens, and I like to redesign my own home several times a year and have acquired a small inventory of pillows, prints, greenery, and florals that I use for my business."

Once you are ready to create your own staging stockpile, there are a number of resources to explore for affordable, good-quality props and furniture:

General Resources

- Antique malls
- Consignment stores
- Craft stores
- Estate sales
- Fabric stores
- Family and friends
- Furniture rental companies
- Garage or yard sales
- Hardware stores
- Hotel furniture liquidators
- Second-hand stores
- Thrift stores

National Retail and Department Stores

- *Bombay & Co. (Canada)*
  www.bombay.ca

- *Bed Bath & Beyond*
  www.bedbathandbeyond.com

- *Cost Plus World Market*
  www.worldmarket.com

- *Costco*
  www.costco.com

- *eBay*
  www.ebay.com

- *Home Outfitters (Canada)*
  www.homeoutfitters.com/en/index.html

- *HomeSense (Canada)*
  www.homesense.ca

- *Ikea*
  www.ikea.com

- *Kirkland's*
  www.kirklands.com

- *Linens 'n Things*
  www.lnt.com

- *Marshalls*
  www.marshallsonline.com

- *Michael's*
  www.michaels.com

- *Overstock.com*
  www.overstock.com

- *Pier 1*
  www.pier1.com

- *Ross Stores*
  www.rossstores.com

- *Sam's Club*
  www.samsclub.com

- *T.J. Maxx*
  www.tjmaxx.com

- *Target*
  www.target.com

- *Tuesday Morning*
  www.tuesdaymorning.com

- *Winners (Canada)*
  www.winners.ca

Buying Items for Clients

Occasionally, you will be asked by your clients to recommend pieces that they can use to stage their home and then later take to their new home. If your commission programs and decorator discounts are already established with local retailers, you'll know exactly where you want to shop. You can fulfill these requests by offering professional shopping services:

- Take clients shopping at your preferred stores or to those stores which will best meet their needs. You should charge an hourly rate for shopping trips, so that the client is encouraged to stay focused on their project. Some decorators also charge their clients a percentage of the total sales made during the outings.

- Act as their personal shopper, or go shopping on their behalf with a predetermined budget. As you purchase items, verify the store's return policy and hold on to all receipts, in case you need to return something. A related service is to borrow items on deposit from a retail showroom with which you have an established relationship. You can then place the items in your client's home for a trial run. If after a day or week, they decide to keep the new item, simply collect payment from the client and pay the retail store for their inventory.

2.3 How to Do Client Consultations

2.3.1 Meeting with Clients

As your business grows, client meetings may end up becoming an every day event. In preparation for this, you should know the dos and don'ts of having a meeting with your customers. One of the most important things to strive for is being punctual to each and every client meeting. The rule of thumb is to be no more than fifteen minutes early or late to an appointment. If you are going to be more than fifteen minutes late, you should always call and let the client know that you are still on your way.

You may find it helpful to practice the following tips with a friend or family member who either needs a consultation or will volunteer to role-play as a client. This practice run will allow you to find your weak points and improve upon them before your first client meeting.

Making a Good Impression With Clients

Gillian Cunningham is a licensed Realtor, Broker, and ASP with Prestique Realty of Plano, Texas, which specializes in the Dallas luxury home market. Her advice on making a good impression with clients:

> "...I believe it is very important for stagers... to market themselves and the value of staging to both potential clients and realtors. To do so, I strongly recommend a stager have a brochure of their services, as well as a portfolio of 'Before & After' photos of homes that have been staged. Remember, presentation is everything. This material must be presented in a very professional manner, especially as one moves up in price point."

You can find more advice about marketing and about creating a portfolio in section 5.2.

Why have a meeting?

From your initial phone conversation, you will know generally what services the client is seeking: home staging, consulting services, or another service you offer. The main purpose of a client meeting (or consultation) is to thoroughly evaluate their need for your services. Additionally, you can see if your traits are a good fit with the homeowner's personality.

A consultation is also an opportunity to build an affinity with a client. You can do this by remarking favorably on their neighborhood, their flowers in the front garden, or a piece of art that greets you in the foyer. There is always something positive, or something you can identify with, in any home. This casual introductory conversation shouldn't last too long though, so only spend about ten minutes on this.

The average initial consultation will probably last about two hours or possibly longer if the whole house is being toured. Be sure to show a portfolio of "Before and After" pictures of your staging transformations, so the client can get a feel for the service and your talent as well.

Qualifying Clients

To ensure early on that potential clients are a good fit for your services, you should evaluate their intentions and their ability to pay. Clients who are willing to shell out a consultation fee for their first meeting will most likely be financially capable of hiring you, and they recognize that your advice is worthy of compensation.

Toni Bouman of Toni B Interiors, a home stager and real estate broker, says that when she first started her business, no one told her "how flaky people were... and how to pre-qualify them by asking questions that both put them at ease and helped me determine if I wanted to work with them."

In general, it is not beneficial to give out free advice in the hopes of landing a bigger job. Even after an initial consultation with a client, you may not see them again. You shouldn't count on future work until you have a signed agreement or contract in hand. Chicago-based home stager, Diana Ezerins, agrees with Toni that "it is critical to pre-screen all prospective clients to ensure they are financially able to afford your services and aren't looking for free information so that they can do amateur staging themselves."

2.3.2 Assessing a Client's Needs

For a home staging consultation, you will need to tour the whole house. Have a notepad or clipboard handy so you can jot down notes on each room. Your client will mention their concerns and thoughts on each space as you tour the home. Sometimes, however, you will need to ask questions in order to get a better feel for the homeowner's needs.

This is also a good time to take "before" photos if the homeowner agrees that this is acceptable. Usually, they are excited to have an image of how their home looked prior to the transformation. If you don't already have one, a digital camera will definitely be a good investment because you can get high quality photos in a short time frame.

Even after touring the house and speaking with the client, there may still be gaps in your notes. You can use a client questionnaire such as the one on the next page to help you gather more information on the project, if needed.

If you haven't already explained the benefits of home staging to your client, this is the perfect time to do so.

Benefits of home staging to share with your client:

- When compared to similar homes on the market, your client's home will stand out to buyers.
- The client's home will likely sell for a higher price, have more offers, or sell faster than it would have without your staging services.
- Real estate agents want to bring buyers to homes they think can be sold easily, and a house that is staged has that move-in-ready feel.

2.3.3 Assessing a Client's Space

When visually scanning a client's dwelling, there are a great number of factors to consider:

- What is not working in this space? Is it the paint, furniture, windows, flooring, or something else?

Sample Client Questionnaire

General Questions

What is the purpose of this home staging project?

How is each room used, or what is each room's function?

Is there a need to accommodate multiple uses in any rooms?

Who uses each room?

Are there any children or pets to consider?

Is there a need for new items or is there a need for rental furniture?

Budgeting and Timeline

What is the client's budget for this project? ________________

When is the home due to be listed? ________________

If cleaning or preparations are necessary prior to the home being staged, when can the client have the work completed?

Will the client need additional services such as cleaning or repairs, or outdoor services?

- Are the room's best features and the focal point being played up or are they hidden?
- Can the room's items be rearranged to enhance the space or can they be used in another room?
- What items from the rest of the house would work in this room?
- Is there a way to make the room function better for its intended purpose?

To help you make the most educated suggestions to your clients, you should know industry terminology and techniques for achieving dynamic design in any space. The rest of this chapter and the next can help you develop your knowledge of design and staging principals.

To assess the client's home, you can use a space assessment checklist such as the one on the next page. Simply write in your impressions of each room in the box, record any issues or problems that you perceive need to be addressed, and write down your recommendations for each.

2.3.4 Presenting a Proposal

After your initial consultation and tour of the property, you are ready to present the client with your recommendations and the proposed fee for your services. A proposal will lay out what services are to be performed and what fees are expected in return for those services. You will probably develop a standard proposal that can be quickly customized for each client and modified as needed for special situations. You can present it in the form of a contract or services agreement (you can see a sample in section 2.3.5).

It's best to present your pricing in general categories or as a lump sum, rather than showing a detailed, itemized list which can be confusing for clients to sort out. Also, they usually want the process to be simple and easy, allowing you to handle all the details. If a client does request a price itemization, you should gladly provide it. You can also recap the benefits of home staging to help sell your proposal.

Sample Home Assessment Form

Client Name		Today's Date	
Client Address		Date of Move	
Client City/ State/ZIP			

	Location/Function	Recommendations
Outside Areas		
1.		
2.		
3.		
Foyer		
Kitchen		
Living Room		
Dining Room		
Bedrooms		
1.		
2.		
3.		
Bathrooms		
1.		
2.		
3.		
Closets/Storage		
1.		
2.		
3.		
Other Rooms and Areas		
1.		
2.		
3.		
Laundry Room		
Basement		

How is an estimate different from a proposal? An estimate is an approximate price that you verbally quote to a client, while mentioning that it is amendable based on the final project details. A proposal, or bid, is a written agreement to complete a job for a specific fee. Make sure you have all the required project information before committing to a proposal. If there is a possibility of additional time or services needed, include the rates for these extras in your proposal notes, service contract, or letter of agreement.

Closing the Deal

After communicating with the client about their needs, you will also have to be an effective salesperson when it comes time to present them with your proposal. You should be comfortable with some basic sales techniques that will help you close the deal:

- Display confidence in yourself and your services. Without acting smugly, you should presume to already have the sale.
- Confirm that you have the household decision-maker at your client meeting. Otherwise, you may end up hearing that they need to talk it over with their spouse, in which case you should follow up with them the next day.
- Pay close attention to the client's response or reaction as you present the proposal. Did they look stunned upon seeing the price? You can always recommend an alternate package to lower the cost.
- Did they show approval as you laid out the proposal? If so, the next step is to have them sign the proposal, contract, or a letter of agreement. A sample letter of agreement is included in section 2.3.5 of this guide as a starting point.
- Request a deposit of one-third or one-half of the total proposed cost for your services. While not absolutely necessary, a deposit can provide you with the peace of mind that you already have part of the payment in hand, and it can be used to buy supplies or pay subcontractors.

Always provide a receipt for deposits. Standard receipt books can be found at most office supply stores. The remainder of the balance should be due when the project is completed. Keep in mind that many states have a three-day right of rescission law. This gives your clients a three-day window in which to call off any order that was sold to them in their home.

Be sure to promptly follow-up with any clients who don't immediately agree to your proposal. See if they've had time to make a decision or if they have any questions about the proposal.

2.3.5 Client Contracts

A contract is vital. It can help avoid misunderstandings by ensuring you and your client have the same expectations of the work to be done. It may also protect you. For example, let's assume you're hired by an executive in a homebuilding company. After you've already signed the contract, the person who hired you leaves the company and is replaced by someone who decides your services are no longer needed. Having a contract in place can help you get paid.

Your contract or agreement should explain what services you will provide for the client and how you are to be paid. Your contract may include all of the following:

- Your name, company name, address and contact information
- The client's name, company name (if applicable), address and contact information
- Description of the services being provided
- When the services will be provided
- Any services not being provided
- Fees, including payment terms, deposits, and reimbursement of expenses
- Cancellation policy
- Signature lines for you and the client

On the pages that follow you will find two sample contracts. You can adapt these contracts to fit your needs. The first is a services agreement that you could adapt for use with a corporate client, such as a real estate agency. It covers a number of areas, such as a liability disclaimer.

The second contract included in this section is a sample engagement letter you might use for a small project with an individual client. You could ask your clients to sign it at your initial meeting, or have them return it to you later.

If any changes need to be made to the original contract, simply fill out a change order or write an addendum to attach to the contract. The specific changes should be explained along with any cost differences, and then all parties should sign off on the document. When it's time to pay the final bill, this extra step will help busy, frazzled homeowners remember the changes they requested.

Besides knowing how to provide contracts to your clients, you should also think about contracts with your subcontractors. Most likely, any service providers you work with will have their own standard professional services contract for you to sign. In those cases where a painter or housecleaning business doesn't have a contract, you might consider developing a basic service agreement which lays out the services, the pay rates, and the professional demeanor expected in client's homes. Section 2.11 will explain in detail about working with contractors.

Before using any contract, make sure you have it reviewed by your lawyer to ensure it protects you and meets your particular needs. For example, even if you will only be working on small projects for individuals, ask your lawyer about including additional clauses in your engagement letter, such as a limitation of liability clause.

Sample Services Agreement

THIS AGREEMENT is made this *[date]* day of *[month]*, 20__.

BETWEEN

[insert name of your client] (the "Client"); and *[insert your name or your company's name]* (the "Home Stager"), collectively referred to as the "Parties."

1.1 Services

The Home Stager shall provide the following services ("Services") to the Client in accordance with the terms and conditions of this Agreement:

[Insert a description of the services here].

1.2 Delivery of the Services

- *Start date:* The Home Stager shall commence the provision of the Services on *[insert date here]*.
- *Completion date:* The Home Stager shall complete the Services by *[insert date here]* ("Completion Date").
- *Key dates:* The Home Stager agrees to provide the following parts of the Services by the specific dates set out below: *[insert dates here if you have agreed to specific milestones]*.

1.3 Fees

As consideration for the provision of the Services by the Home Stager, the fees for the provision of the Services are *[insert fees here]* ("Fees").

The Client shall pay for the Home Stager's out-of-pocket expenses including *[insert here]* and other expenses as agreed by the Parties.

1.4 Payment

The Client agrees to pay the Fees to the Home Stager on the following dates:

[insert dates and terms, e.g. 50% deposit payable before work begins; also specify whether the price will be paid in one payment, in installments or upon completion of specific milestones].

The Home Stager shall invoice the Client for the Services that it has provided to the Client *[monthly/weekly/after the Completion*

Date]. The Client shall pay such invoices *[upon receipt/within 30 days of receipt]* from the Home Stager.

Any charges payable under this Agreement are exclusive of any applicable taxes or other fees charged by a government body and such shall be payable by the Client to the Home Stager in addition to all other charges payable hereunder.

1.5 Warranty

The Home Stager represents and warrants that it will perform the Services with reasonable skill and care.

1.6 Limitation of Liability

Subject to the Client's obligation to pay the Fees to the Home Stager, either party's liability arising directly out of its obligations under this Agreement and every applicable part of it shall be limited in aggregate to the Fees.

The Home Stager assumes no liability due to the quality of items or services purchased for the Client.

1.7 Term and Termination

This Agreement shall be effective on the date hereof and shall continue until the completion date stated in section 1.2 unless terminated sooner.

If the Client terminates this agreement for any reason before the scheduled completion date, the Client will reimburse the Home Stager for all outstanding fees and out-of-pocket expenses.

1.8 Relationship of the Parties

The Parties acknowledge and agree that the Services performed by the Home Stager, its employees, sub-contractors, or agents shall be as an independent contractor and that nothing in this Agreement shall be deemed to constitute a partnership, joint venture, or otherwise between the parties.

1.9 Confidentiality

Neither Party will disclose any information of the other which comes into its possession under or in relation to this Agreement and which is of a confidential nature.

1.10 Miscellaneous

The failure of either party to enforce its rights under this Agreement at any time for any period shall not be construed as a waiver of such rights.

If any part, term or provision of this Agreement is held to be illegal or unenforceable neither the validity or enforceability of the remainder of this Agreement shall be affected.

This Agreement constitutes the entire understanding between the Parties and supersedes all prior representations, negotiations or understandings.

Neither Party shall be liable for failure to perform any obligation under this Agreement if the failure is caused by any circumstances beyond its reasonable control, including but not limited to acts of god, war, or industrial dispute.

This Agreement shall be governed by the laws of the jurisdiction in which the Client is located.

Agreed by the Parties hereto:

Signed by: ____________________________________

On behalf of: ____________________________________
[the Client]

Signed by: ____________________________________

On behalf of: ____________________________________
[the Home Stager]

Sample Engagement Letter

[Your Business Name]
[Address]
[City, State, Zip]
[Business Phone]
[Business Fax]
[Business Email]

[Date]

[Client Name]
[Client Address]
[Client Phone]

Thank you for choosing [your business name] for your home staging project. The following agreement details the terms and conditions of this project. Please keep a copy for your records.

Summary of work to be done at your residence:

[insert summary here]

My fee for the services described above is $______, plus applicable sales tax.

If there are any additions or changes to this agreement, *[your business name]* will issue an amended agreement detailing the new information and any applicable fees for you to approve.

Payment of the base fee must be made as follows: (check one)

- ❑ Payment due in full upon completion of services.
- ❑ 50% deposit due upon signing this agreement and remaining 50% due upon completion of services.

Sincerely,
[Your Name]
Owner, *[Your Business Name]*

ACCEPTED AND AGREED:
By: ________________________ Date: __________

Sample Change Order

[Your Company Name]

[Date]

[Client Name]
[Client Address]
[Client Phone]

Description of Change:

[insert description of change]

Price Increase or Decrease: $ *[insert dollar amount]*

I, *[homeowner]*, concur that the stated change items are accurate and were asked for by me. I will compensate for the variation in price if it is more than the original bill. I approve *[your business name or a subcontractor's business name]* to make the changes described above.

ACCEPTED AND AGREED:

______________________________	______________
[the Client]	Date
______________________________	______________
[the Home Stager]	Date

2.4 An Overview of How to Stage a Home

Staging a house for the real estate market is fundamentally different from decorating for everyday living. In fact, home staging is almost the opposite of decorating because it is about neutralizing décor and removing a client's identity from a home so that it appeals to buyers of all tastes and preferences. Your staging client, the seller, must detach from their house and begin to see it as a commodity to be skillfully packaged and marketed to realtors and buyers.

Real estate agents show buyers those houses with the best chances of selling, so a staged home will move to the top of their showing list. For the most part, homebuyers want a move-in-ready house that is clutter free, sparkling clean, and full of sunshine. A staged home will provide all these things, and buyers are willing to pay more to get it. Your job as a home stager is to see a house from the buyer's point of view and help your clients to do the same.

Understanding the Buyer's Point of View

Picture yourself as a homebuyer. You and your real estate agent drive up to a potential house. You quickly scan the front yard and the house's exterior. Already, you know if you want to go inside or not.

You make your way past the front porch and through the front door. As you catch a glimpse of the foyer and rooms beyond, you're probably already making your decision about this house. Every small detail along the way reinforces or tears down your first impression of the property.

This exercise of putting yourself in the buyer's shoes is one of the basic elements of being a home stager. That's exactly what you should be trying to accomplish as a stager: bringing out the best in each home you encounter.

Each area of the house, including the exterior, needs to impact the viewer in a positive way. Below is an introduction to creating appeal for each area and room, from a buyer's perspective. The remaining sections of this chapter will provide more details about how to stage these areas.

Outside Areas

Since the front yard is one of the initial areas a buyer will see, this area must make a great first impression. Side and back yard areas will also be scrutinized by buyers. These areas should be tidy, well-groomed, and add value to the house.

Foyer

The home's entrance hall will be the first interior space seen by buyers. An uncluttered, welcoming foyer is essential.

Living Rooms

Before

This uninviting, vacant living room makes it difficult for a buyer to visualize furniture in the space.❖

After

After staging, the fireplace stands out as the focal point. The neutral furniture is arranged to create a conversation area while pops of color from the accessories tie the space together and add visual punch.❖

Staging by Charlene Storozuk, Home Design Consultant of Dezigner Digz™ and Regional Vice-President, Canada, for the Real Estate Staging Association, Burlington, Ontario, Canada, www.dezignerdigz.com.

Living Rooms

Before

This empty space makes it hard for homebuyers to picture using the room and what to place between the two windows. ❖

After

The upscale family room now has furniture arranged with the fireplace and flat screen as a focal point. Two chairs create a conversation area with the sofa, while a cabinet and painting create harmony with the two windows. ❖

Staging by Robin Rosen, President of Stageffect, Inc., Chappaqua, New York, www.stageffect.com. Photography by Peter Krupenye Photography.

Living Rooms

Before

This vacant home has unique architectural features which need to be showcased. ❖

After

A sofa and two chairs make the most of the main sitting area while keeping the patio view open. A reading nook has been established in the adjacent room to show the versatility of the space.❖

Staging by Kim Kapellusch, Prepared to Sell, Valencia, CA, www.preparedtosellstaging.com. Photography by Steve Clemons, www.steveclemonsphotography.com.

Bedrooms

Before

Old-fashioned décor and worn carpet drag down this bedroom. ❖

After

Removing the carpet added instant value, along with fresh paint and new bedding. This bedroom is now a master suite with a reading nook and stylish drapes. ❖

Staging by Darla Rowley, owner of IMPACT! Interior Design Solutions and Accredited Staging Professional™, Royal Oak, Michigan, www.impactids.com.

Bedrooms

Before

Potential buyers are left guessing how to make the most of this bedroom's features. ❖

After

A luxury suite has been brought to life with fashionable yet neutral furnishings and accessories. The bed is a pleasing focal point as the fireplace gets cozy with two slipper chairs. ❖

Staging by Robin Rosen, President of Stageffect, Inc., Chappaqua, New York, www.stageffect.com. Photography by Peter Krupenye Photography.

Kitchens

Before

With appliances cluttering up the space, this kitchen seems short on countertops. ❖

After

Clear counters open up the space while simple red flowers draw the eye to the charming view above the sink. ❖

Staging by Annie Pinsker-Brown, Stage to Sell, Low Angeles, CA, www.StageToSell.biz.

Kitchens

Before

Even with the strong bones of this kitchen, it feels unwelcoming when left vacant. ❖

After

Buyers can now easily imagine their lifestyle in this amazing chef's kitchen. Seating options are now clearly defined while food accessories add life to the décor. ❖

Staging by Robin Rosen, President of Stageffect, Inc., Chappaqua, New York, www.stageffect.com. Photography by Peter Krupenye Photography.

Kitchens

Before

An outmoded countertop and 1950's cabinets left buyers with the impression the kitchen needed major remodeling. ❖

After

White paint and brushed nickel hardware modernize the cabinetry as new laminate countertops add immediate value. Removing the ivy wallpaper border and applying a fresh coat of paint makes the whole room look updated. ❖

Staging by Darla Rowley, owner of IMPACT! Interior Design Solutions and Accredited Staging Professional™, Royal Oak, Michigan, www.impactids.com.

Offices

Before

This home office was suffering from too many wires, looming overhead shelves, and crowded furniture. ❖

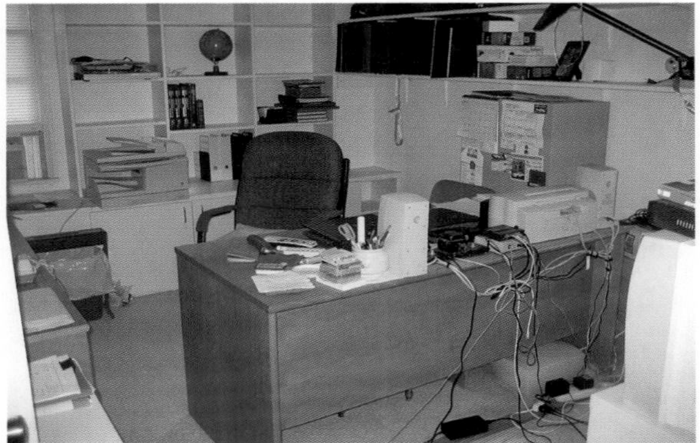

After

A streamlined office space focuses on the built-in bookcase. ❖

Staging by Annie Pinsker-Brown, Stage to Sell, Low Angeles, CA, www.StageToSell.biz.

Bathrooms

Before

This home had been labeled "the foil wallpaper condo" by realtors. Chaotic wallcoverings are sure to scare away home shoppers.❖

After

Removal of the wallpaper and an updated paint color create a modern bathroom complete with a new light fixture. These cost-effective renovations allowed the original vanity and fixtures to remain in place.❖

Staging by Darla Rowley, owner of IMPACT! Interior Design Solutions and Accredited Staging Professional™, Royal Oak, Michigan, www.impactids.com.

Bathrooms

Before

A nondescript master bathroom is definitely not romancing potential buyers. ❖

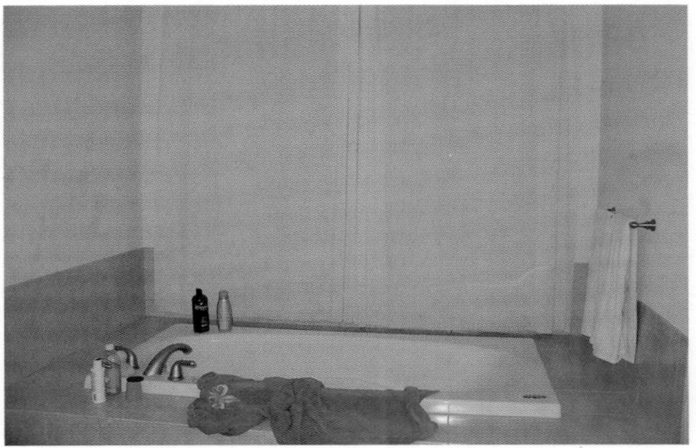

After

A few basic decorative accessories and tassel tiebacks on the drapes transform this space into a spa getaway with a view. ❖

Staging by Darla Rowley, owner of IMPACT! Interior Design Solutions and Accredited Staging Professional™, Royal Oak, Michigan, www.impactids.com.

Dining Rooms

Before

The dated furniture and ethnic accessories would likely turn off many buyers. ❖

After

By slipcovering the chairs, removing the table cloth, and switching out the art, it's suddenly a very neutral space which any family could enjoy. ❖

Staging by Annie Pinsker-Brown, Stage to Sell, Low Angeles, CA, www.StageToSell.biz.

Dining Rooms

Before

A dining room bogged down with personal accessories and surplus furniture pieces will distract buyers. ❖

After

Family photos and clutter were removed from the room. Eye-catching accessories create balance with the furniture and wall color in this well-appointed formal dining space. ❖

Staging by Robin Rosen, President of Stageffect, Inc., Chappaqua, New York, www.stageffect.com. Photography by Peter Krupenye Photography.

Foyers

Before

The fabulous features of this empty foyer might be missed with nothing to hold buyer's attention. ❖

After

Furniture pieces and artwork establish a sophisticated, welcoming space which makes buyers want to see more. ❖

Staging by Robin Rosen, President of Stageffect, Inc., Chappaqua, New York, www.stageffect.com. Photography by Peter Krupenye Photography.

Curb Appeal - Home Front Exteriors

Before

No one will purchase a house they can't see. The first impression of the front entry is a significant location that sets the tone for the buyer. ❖

After

Curb appeal of this Tudor treasure has been improved by removing overgrown shrubberies and landscaping. An updated front door is installed for a more contemporary look. ❖

Staging by Julie Dana, The Home Stylist, Accredited Staging Professional™, East Aurora, NY, and author of ***The Complete Idiot's Guide to Staging Your Home to Sell****, www.thehomestylist.com.*

Other

Before

A vacant sunroom is valuable additional square footage and it should be treated as such.❖

After

Several seating areas are established which are perfect for relaxing or entertaining.❖

Staging by Robin Rosen, President of Stageffect, Inc., Chappaqua, New York, www.stageffect.com. Photography by Peter Krupenye Photography.

Kitchen

Considered by many to be the heart of a home, the kitchen is best when it is sparkling clean, free of clutter, and light-filled. Appliances should be in working order, the inside of the refrigerator should be spotless, and the pantry should be orderly.

Living Room

Some clients will have a formal living room and a family room or den. All the same, these rooms are where the new homeowners will be spending a lot of their time with family and friends. Buyers want living areas that feel roomy and relaxing.

Dining Room

Whether it is a cozy breakfast nook or a formal entertaining space, dining areas should be comfortable and functional. Two to four place settings or a small tablescape will make these rooms more tangible to buyers.

Bedrooms

When staging master bedrooms, children's rooms, and guest rooms, keep in mind that the most desirable bedrooms are serene and restful. They should be staged simply—uncrowded with few distracting elements.

Bathrooms

Homebuyers are looking for bathrooms that are squeaky clean, uncluttered, and working properly. Master bathrooms can be staged with a little luxury in mind, since a spa-like feel is popular. A few fluffy towels and a bathtub vignette are all you need.

Closets

The most sought-after trait for any closet is spaciousness, since its main function is as a storage space. Have your clients pack up nearly all closet contents so only their essential items remain. Then stage the closet with organization and space in mind.

Other Rooms and Areas

Many homes will have additional rooms to stage such as studies, offices, libraries, game rooms, or music rooms. Since these rooms are likely to have a lot of books and paperwork, encourage your clients to pack almost all of it for the move. Then these rooms can be staged with a few key accessories to show off their function. Hallways, utility areas, laundry rooms, and basements should be extremely well-lit and safely organized.

Once you understand what the buyer is looking for, you can carry out the actual staging for your client. The first step in the process of adding buyer appeal to a client's home is organizing and decluttering the house. In the next section we'll take you through this process step-by-step and show you how this process helps to depersonalize the home, making it possible for buyers to imagine themselves living there.

2.5 Organizing and Decluttering

One of the key things buyers are looking for is an uncluttered house. This is the first phase in the home staging process, so you should encourage your clients to start packing early for their move. This will ensure that a great deal of their personal items and any clutter are removed at the beginning of the staging process and make your job that much easier.

Jason Maxwell of Equity Enhancers advises stagers to "always honor your clients and their possessions, as it is their life and personality you will ultimately be removing from the home when you stage it, turning it into a house that is a marketable product." With staging, you are clearing the space so potential buyers can imagine themselves living in the home. Remind your clients that their house is for sale, not their belongings, so the focus will be on the real estate itself.

Although much of the clutter clearing will be a task your client will be assigned to complete prior to the staging day, you can also offer this service as an addition to your staging package or refer clients to a contractor who specializes in organization. Even after your client completes their clutter cleanup, there will probably be a few remaining items that you will need to remove during the staging process (more on that later in this section).

2.5.1 Identifying Clutter

Clutter can encompass a wide variety of items such as junk mail, newspapers, office paperwork, periodicals, excess furniture, area rugs, surplus accessories, and kitchen gadgets, to name a few. Basically, clutter is anything that creates a messy, muddled, confusing, or chaotic feeling in your client's indoor or outdoor spaces.

As you evaluate each room during a consultation, make note of what items need to be cleared out and what can stay for staging purposes. This list of items can be given to the homeowner as part of your recommendations. You will probably be staging a property with select pieces of your client's furniture and accessories as well as your own staging props which you either own or will rent. Take a look at the color section in the center of this book to see an example of how to de-clutter a room.

On the day of staging, you can take another mental inventory to make sure that all unnecessary items are removed and that you have all the pieces necessary for staging each room. In all residences, there are zones that seem to accumulate clutter rather quickly and easily. Here are a few problematic areas in your client's home where clutter issues are commonly found.

Kitchens

Your client's kitchen is one of the key features that homebuyers will be most interested in seeing. Frequently occurring kitchen clutter issues that should be corrected include:

- excess gadgets or small appliances
- untidy recipe books
- refrigerator door "art" and fridge magnets
- disorganized pantries
- plate and knickknack collections
- messy windowsills
- too many area rugs

The kitchen is also an area where incoming junk mail, newspapers, and periodicals tend to stack up.

Bookshelves

Shelves and bookcases tend to become overwhelmed when too many books and accessories are displayed. In fact, one problem you'll encounter is shelves not being used to display items but rather to store them in an unsightly or crowded manner.

Children's Rooms

Children's bedrooms and playrooms are often times filled to capacity with toys, dolls, stuffed animals, and items on the walls. All that's required here is to box up or donate items that can't be stored neatly in a closet or toy chest. The children should be involved in this cleanup process so they understand it's only temporary and so they can take an active role in choosing what will stay in their room.

Entertainment Centers

Many entertainment centers house a television in addition to numerous DVDs, videos, books, accessories, and photo frames. All these items can lead to a cluttered-looking cabinet or wall unit, so recommend that almost all of these items be packed away early.

Offices, Studies, and Computer Rooms

Any room where bills are paid or work is done on a computer can show signs of disorganization. Most of the time, this clutter will consist of paperwork that needs to be filed or thrown out, computer gadgets or supplies, newspapers, and magazines. Your client has probably wanted to organize their office space for a while, and there's no better time than when you are staging their house. It will be one less thing for them to worry about when moving day arrives.

Basements

Some basements are simply overflowing with many items that would be good candidates for a garage sale. A basement that is clutter-free will add square footage to your client's house and leave room for buyers to imagine its potential uses. The popularity of home theater rooms has many people looking for a large space for just such a purpose. Another popular remodeling project is to transform a basement into a game room retreat for teenager or adult use.

Garages and Patios

Outdoor spaces can become the collection point for an ample assortment of items. Patio and garage clutter can consist of empty flower containers, lumber, children's toys, sports equipment, cans of paint, gardening supplies, and tools. While most of these things can be put in a garage sale, thrown out, or put in storage, there will be items that your clients may need while their house is on the market. They should keep these areas as cleared out as possible and neatly store any necessary equipment.

2.5.2 Disposing of Clutter

Your client can keep from feeling overwhelmed by starting early in the home selling process and working on one room per day. Bring assembled cardboard boxes, plastic storage bins, packing materials, and trash bags into each room. Sort all the room's contents into items for charity, items to throw out, items to pack, and items to sell (not all clients will be interested in this last option). Your client can use the cardboard boxes or plastic bins for items that will be moved with them to their new home.

Once a box is full, it can be taped up and labeled. Use the trash bags for the items to be thrown out, the charitable items, and the items to be sold. The room's furnishings should also be categorized the same way and moved accordingly. Key leftover items can now be used for staging the house.

Depending on local regulations, there are different considerations for the trash items. Most cities offer a bulk trash pick-up or drop-off option, so your client will need to determine the best choice for them.

Charitable organizations will frequently have on-going collection truck schedules, so your client can call and schedule a pick-up time. Also, some charities have convenient drop-off bins outside their collection offices.

For any items set aside to be sold, your client can host a garage sale. However, it will be much quicker to donate the items and take a tax deduction by getting a receipt for their contributions. They will likely have enough on their plate without a garage sale to manage, but some clients may still prefer this option.

All the items packed in boxes for your client's move should ideally be taken to off-site storage. This will optimize the space in their closets and garage so buyers can see plenty of potential storage when viewing your client's house. If a few tidy boxes need to be stored in the garage or in a spare room, this should be done as neatly and inconspicuously as possible.

2.5.3 Removing Personal or Offensive Items

Certain items need to be removed from your client's home not only because they may be cluttering the space, but because they are too personal or specific to the home seller. You want to make a client's house resemble a builder's model home which features no personal or offensive items whatsoever.

A model home's décor makes it easy for a variety of potential buyers to feel at ease and envision their personal items in the house. In order to achieve the same effect with a lived-in home, it will be up to you, as a home stager, to gently and sensitively inform your clients what must go. You can do this by explaining why each item should go and reminding them to see their house as a buyer would see it.

Family photos are considered clutter mainly because buyers have a hard time considering a home as being their own when they see the client's personal photos everywhere they look. It makes buyers uncomfortable and sends a message that a seller isn't ready to move. Your client should include family photos and albums in the items that they pack ahead of time and put in storage. Remind them that this is only a temporary arrangement and that their cherished family photos will be back up in no time in their new home.

Other personal items that should be removed include jewelry, shoes, toiletries, and perfume bottles which can create clutter when left in view. Plus, your client does not want any of their expensive items to tempt the wrong person. Some essential bath and beauty items can be kept under the sink or in a nice basket, but a mountain of lotion bottles and personal care items will only make buyers uncomfortable.

Any items that may be offensive to potential home buyers should be removed from your client's home. For example, posters of scantily clad women adorning a teenage boy's room or the garage would not be appropriate for a staged home. Remind your clients that selling their house is not the time to make social, political, or religious statements.

TIP: If a client refuses to remove problematic items, you should stipulate these in your contract and get them to sign-off on it. That way, you will have written proof that they chose not to follow all of your recommendations. This little step will protect you if a client ever demands a refund because their home did not sell as quickly or for as much as expected.

2.5.4 Handling Collections and Hobbies

Collections

Your clients should box up any items they don't want eyeballed by the crowd of strangers who will wander through their house. Expensive items or collectibles are not needed to impress buyers, so have your client carefully pack and store them. This is especially important for small, easily removable items like heirloom silver cutlery.

However, you can use several key pieces from a collection of accessories in staging the home. Keep in mind the ancient Greeks' fondness for grouping objects in sets of odd numbers like one and three. For example, one gorgeous glass bowl on a coffee table is enough when staging a home just like a grouping of three oil paintings is sufficient to dress up a large wall.

Hobby-Related Clutter

A client's home may have items pertaining to hobbies of any or all the family members. Maybe someone in the house likes to sew or builds scale models of wooden ships. We all have enjoyable hobbies of some sort that take up space in our homes while frequently contributing to clutter. This may be fine while your client lives in their house, but hobby-related clutter is not something that will help stage their home for buyers.

All hobby-related items should be packed up early in preparation for the move, especially if these activities are taking over a bedroom or spare room. These rooms will show better if staged as a guest room or study since these are more commonly sought by buyers. In a large house, there may be a music room in addition to plenty of bedrooms, a study, or other spare rooms. In this case, it makes sense to stage this room using one or two of the client's musical instruments.

For stubborn clients, gently explain that they're selling their house, not the stuff in their house. Clutter, no matter how special or artistic it may be, will only sidetrack buyers from seeing the home clearly and with the least amount of bias.

2.5.5 Storage: Closets, Garages, and Attics

Your clients may need to use some interior space for storing boxes or items not being displayed in the staged house. This is okay to some extent, but a client should keep their stored items as neat and compact as possible. The ideal situation is for any boxes and spare furnishings to be stored off-site. Since buyers almost always size up the garage and closets in a home, the attic would be a better choice for a temporary storage spot.

Spacious closets are something buyers want, so encourage clients to sort their clothing and shoe collections. They can pack up unneeded items or give things to charity, but either way an orderly closet will look larger. Any broken rods or shelves should be repaired or replaced.

Likewise, an organized garage looks more appealing to buyers who may be seeking extra space for hobbies or to store vehicles. Garage floors that have cracks or oil stains should be restored and cleaned. A client may be able to accomplish this in one step by applying cement floor paint or a special garage floor epoxy coating.

Off-Site Storage

As mentioned earlier in this chapter, your clients will be packing early for their move in order to help ready the house for staging. Of course, they will need a place to store all those boxes and extra furniture until they are ready to move, and usually a staged home will make this day arrive sooner. While there may be room for a few boxes to stay in the house, off-site storage will generally be required. In these cases, your clients will need to rent a storage unit or have a storage pod dropped off at their house.

Self-storage units (sometimes called mini storage) are available in almost every city with month-to-month rental plans. It is a good idea for your clients to opt for a climate controlled building, as this stable environment will protect their cherished photos and other delicate items. Also, self-storage facilities will often have areas available for parking any boats, recreational vehicles, cars, or motorcycles that may be cluttering your client's garage or carport.

A storage pod is a portable storage unit that can be dropped off at your client's house. Your client can then fill this weather-proof unit at their own pace. When they are finished, the storage pod will be picked up and kept in a storage facility or delivered to the destination of their choice. For more information about storage pods, check out **www.publicstorage.com** and **www.pods.com**.

2.6 Cleaning and Repairs

Another key component that buyers are in search of is an exceptionally clean house. Each staged house must be spotless, sparkling, squeaky-clean, and pass the white glove test. Not that you will literally put on a white glove and run your fingers along the baseboards, but you should feel confident that the client's house would be able to pass such a test.

It is a necessity that your client's house be spick and span to make an impression on buyers. We all know this isn't how most people live on an everyday basis, but the client's home is a product in a very competitive market, and it needs to stand above the rest.

It's also crucial that your client's house be in great working order. A few wobbly cabinet doors, a broken toilet seat, and damaged countertops or tiles may be enough to put off most buyers. These little details can help or hurt your client's chances of selling their home quickly and for the highest possible amount.

If you need help making sure a house is in tip top shape, try a service like Merry Maids (**www.merrymaids.com**) or Mr. Handyman (**www.mrhandyman.com**).

2.6.1 Identifying Trouble Spots

As you tour a client's home, you should note any areas that will call for extra cleaning or require repairs. Buyers will be looking for trouble spots so they can reduce their offer or ask for an allowance to replace or repair items. Here are some general things to look for:

- Areas not cleaned on a regular basis will almost certainly need some special attention.
- Fireplaces may have ashes to scoop or vacuum out, as well as sooty bricks to scrub or paint.
- Baseboards might need dusting, scrubbing or painting to make them look crisp and fresh.
- Some areas in a home collect dust and dirt but are not in plain view all the time such as window sills, blinds, drapes, appliance tops, range hoods, ovens, ceilings, vents, fans, and cabinet tops.

If a buyer happens to be six feet tall, you want them to see spotless surfaces everywhere they may look.

Floors, carpets, and rugs should also be in tip-top shape. Your client should replace, repair, or professionally clean all floor surfaces. Having move-in ready flooring is a much better option than offering or negotiating an allowance while the house is on the market.

Smells will keep a house from being shown or being sold. These uncomfortable odors can be from any number of sources including cooking, pets, bed-wetting children, mildew, or smoking inside the house.

Be sensitive to your client's feelings as you bring up smells in their house, but also remember that they are paying you to tell them things about their house that no one else will. Even though a client may already know certain odors are a problem, they may have become immune to other lingering smells.

Pets

Our beloved animal friends bring so much joy to life, but they can create issues when a client's house is on the market. After sorting out any pet-related smells and stains, we can now deal with the pets themselves. Since a potential buyer could be allergic to or afraid of certain animals, you should recommend that your clients confine or remove pets during showings. This is especially the case for any reptiles or insects.

Your client can secure pets in a kennel or spare room, have a friend or neighbor pet-sit, or take them to a pet daycare. Also suggest that any pet supplies, such as water and food bowls, be moved to a less noticeable place. This reduces clutter in common areas and makes walking paths safer.

In addition to cleanliness and odors, any areas needing repairs will have to be addressed. Your clients should always fix all of the simple and low-cost repairs such as replacing light bulbs, tightening loose door handles, cleaning tile grout, and repairing drippy faucets. Repairs requiring a little more effort or cost will probably end up being a good investment on the client's part because they will get higher offers for their home.

If your client needs help with cleaning or repairs, you can offer these extra services as add-ons to your staging package. You can also bring in subcontractors and specialists to provide these services. Your client may already have people they use for repairs or housecleaning, but you can also refer them to trusted companies for a referral fee. A cost-benefit analysis should be done by the client since they know their budget, but you should definitely recommend which items ought to be fixed.

2.6.2 Masking Damage

Some items require a large investment in order to repair, or maybe there's just not time to get all the repairs done. Occasionally, you'll need to use a few shortcuts in order to mask damage in a client's house.

In Walls

Holes in drywall or cracks in walls can be patched up and filled with spackle in a few minutes. Once painted, these imperfections will be hard to spot. To fully repair larger size holes, a replacement piece of drywall material or a drywall patch kit may be needed.

When asked about her favorite industry secret, Joanne Hans, owner of A Perfect Placement, reveals that the "Mr. Clean Magic Eraser…may take the place of a new paint job!" The Magic Eraser and its generic-brand counterparts are part of a new class of water-activated foam cleaning sponges that can remove dirt and grime from virtually any surface.

In Flooring

A quick fix for holes, burns, or stubborn stains in carpeting is to cut out the damaged section and replace it with a matching piece from the back corner of a closet or from a leftover carpet roll the homeowner may have in storage. In a pinch, you can probably find a close match at a carpeting store. They will have glues for attaching the new piece to the existing carpet padding. Carpet installers also have expertise in patching holes, so call one if you have any uncertainties. Don't cut the original carpet until you know for sure there is an exact or nearly identical match.

Missing or damaged linoleum, ceramic tiles, and sheet vinyl flooring can be fixed in much the same way as carpet holes. First see if the homeowner has extra tile, and if not, see if the pattern is still available at the retail level or from the manufacturer. You may need a tile specialist to make this repair go smoothly.

If heavy furniture has been moved recently leaving indents or lines on the carpeting, place ice cubes on the compressed carpet areas and let them melt. Come back later and fluff up the indented sections, using your fingers or a carpet rake.

On Furniture

Furniture stain pens are indispensable for masking scratches or damage on wooden furniture, wood floors, and wood paneling. These stain-filled markers are available at most hardware stores in several wood tones, so it's a good idea to have one of each color in your arsenal. Be sure your client is on board with the application of stain pens before using them.

Sharpie® permanent markers are available in a rainbow of colors and in many tip sizes. Even though these colorful markers should be used sparingly, they can help mask scrapes or damage on almost any surface such as walls, carpeting, rugs, furniture, wood, leather, and fabric. Once again, ensure that your client is okay with the use of markers and apply them in moderation.

In Bathrooms

For extremely damaged or outdated surfaces in bathrooms and kitchens, your clients should consider an affordable re-glazing and resurfacing process such as Perma-Glaze® (**www.permaglaze.com**) or Miracle Method® (**www.miraclemethod.com**). First, the surface is cleaned and any chips or scratches are repaired. Then, numerous layers of resins or coatings are applied to the surface, producing a durable finish that's available in glossy or matte finish custom colors. This process can be used on various surfaces and fixtures including countertops, bathtubs, showers, vanities, sinks, cabinets, and ceramic tiles. The whole transformation is complete in a few hours for about $500, but the costs can be more or less depending on how many surfaces are being done.

Custom-molded acrylic liners are another quick fix for troubled tubs and showers. These liners are either custom molded to fit over existing fixtures or installed as stock panel pieces for the fastest turnaround. Bath Fitter (**www.bathfitter.com**) provides liners to all of North America.

Now that the home has been successfully decluttered and cleaned, it's time to start thinking about decorating.

2.7 Decorating the Rooms

After the clutter is gone, and the cleaning is done, you've arrived at the most enjoyable part of home staging – decorating the rooms to enhance the home's best features. In this section we'll explore how to stage effectively beginning with choosing a design theme (also known as a design concept).

2.7.1 Design Theme or Concept

When staging a client's home, the overall outcome will be more pleasing if a design theme or concept is followed. There are several ways to come up with a design theme for each situation. Maybe a client will have a stunning collection of antiques or a room full of Asian inspired treasures. Immediately, you have something you can work into a suitable theme.

Sometimes, you won't see a theme with the furnishings or accessories until you've seen the entire house because many times pieces are split up. Whether it's a collection of beautiful French Limoges china or a set of custom upholstered sofa and chairs, they should be displayed together for maximum impact.

Another source of inspiration can be the house itself or even the neighborhood. Is it a lovely Tudor style home or a casual beach house? All of these clues will tell you what design concept will work for your client. If you are asked to stage an empty home, then the only sources of inspiration will be the home and its surroundings. You can then rent or bring in your own furniture and accessories to suit the chosen design theme.

Some of the most widely accepted themes to help showcase a house include traditional, contemporary, and casual.

Traditional

If you are staging an upscale home in a country club neighborhood, then most likely you will need to carry out a formal, traditional design plan. If the client's furniture is up to this task, then using what they have will work. You may end up bringing in a few additional luxury items since this type of neighborhood will attract a buyer with high expectations, or someone who is willing and able to upgrade their lifestyle to "the good life" expecting comfort and luxury.

This might be a good opportunity to use a "romantic retreat" theme where champagne and fruit are displayed in the fridge or on the kitchen island along with strategically placed glowing candles by the bathtub with a dozen red roses. The traditional theme will also be popular in many other areas with varying price points, so let the home's architectural design, the neighborhood atmosphere, and occasionally the client's furnishings be your guide.

Contemporary

Contemporary design themes are becoming more well-liked. Many times, this theme is dependent on a home designed in a modern or even mid-century modern architectural style. An extremely traditional home is hardly ever decorated and furnished as a clean-lined modern or minimalist interior. However, some traditional clients will have a pleasant, eclectic mix of belongings that includes a few modern pieces.

If you come across a home featuring modern or contemporary architecture, that element should be played up to a reasonable extent. Most buyers coming to see a home in a neighborhood featuring clean-lined modern exteriors are probably looking for the same on the interior of a home.

Casual

Another general design theme that can be used to unify a home is a casual concept. This might include a "family haven" theme where the interior and exterior are easy to maintain and feature kid-friendly features like a nice backyard or a swimming pool. The casual theme can also be employed for beach houses, lake houses, cabins, or other recreational homes.

In an average suburban neighborhood, a casual theme might be desirable when displayed as a laid-back version of a traditional design. For example, a beautiful sofa upholstered in denim or leather rather than a silken fabric would give a more relaxed vibe to the design. This casual design theme might also be attractive to young home buyers in a starter neighborhood who don't want a traditional or formal home.

Choosing the Design Theme

Choosing a design theme or concept is all about understanding the home's architecture, having familiarity with the neighborhood, and knowing what features buyers in that area are looking for in a home. Local real estate agents should be able to help supply some of this information. Once you have chosen the design theme, you can then apply it to each of the room's elements, which are described below.

2.7.2 Walls

As the backdrop for your client's artwork, furniture, and accessories, wall treatments are significant when staging a residence. For a house being readied for the real estate market, keeping color palettes neutral is necessary. This typically means that walls should be a light neutral color such as ivory, off-white, beige, tan, or cream. Avoid a cold white and instead go for a warmer ivory or cream which has a touch of yellow or red to warm it up.

Your clients may ask for paint color recommendations, so you should have some suggestions that are appropriate for staging scenarios. You may also get questions about other wall finishes and even wallpaper. You should be familiar with the terminology and techniques involved with these various wall treatments:

Wallpaper

Wallpaper in one form or another has been in use for centuries. In the last few years, it has surged in popularity and is being requested more often. Grass cloth and textured wallpapers will add dimension and texture to walls. For bathrooms and kitchens, suggest vinyl wallpaper which stands up better to moisture.

Special wallpaper murals and cut-out designs are now available, so it's easy for anyone to have the look of a hand-painted fresco. You can also recommend that a client's existing wallpaper be painted, if removing it is not feasible. Just make sure the wallpaper is secure, use a stain-blocking primer, and paint away.

Paint

Paint is an inexpensive way to give a room an immediate facelift. There are hundreds of stock colors available at most hardware and paint stores, but colors can also be custom mixed to match any surface or object. Using a primer under new paint is a must if you are choosing a dark color (especially red) or if you are applying a light color over a darker color.

Paint is available in several residential finishes:

- Flat paint has a matte finish and hides flaws in the wall surface, but it is not as easily cleaned as other finishes. Its best applications are ceilings, master bedrooms, and low traffic rooms.
- Eggshell or satin paint has a low luster finish that is easily cleaned making it suitable for active zones like hallways, children's rooms, and living rooms.
- Semi-gloss paint features a hard-wearing finish that is perfect for trim, kitchens, bathrooms, utility rooms, and doors.
- High-gloss paint has a very tough, glossy finish which is suitable for cabinets and trim.

Decorative and faux finishes include numerous paint techniques used to add texture to interior walls. These applications typically use two or more paint colors layered by glazing, sponging, color washing, spattering, stippling, or ragging. A faux finish involves applying paint to suggest another surface such as wood, marble, stone, or granite.

Another popular decorative finish is Venetian plaster which calls for an extremely smooth wall surface that is then troweled with plaster and painted to have a glossy, textured look. Painted murals also fall into the decorative finishes category.

Artwork

Artwork is something that can be very personal when it is part of a client's collection, but it can also be a terrific mood enhancer in a staged house. Artwork encompasses a range of wall décor items including paintings, mirrors, photographs, prints, screens, tapestries, sconces, and plaques. Here are a few techniques for planning and arranging your client's wall space:

Create Groupings

Group wall décor items by similar features such as their frame, material, color, finish, shape, theme, or style. Artwork should also complement the furniture using the same criteria. For example, a collection of prints in wooden frames will be a great match to an oak armoire.

To create a gallery of wall art, start by laying out the art in a large rectangle or square shape with space in the middle. The outer edges of the frames will create the outer edge of the rectangle. Then fill in the middle of the arrangement with more artwork. You can plan and visualize artwork displays by arranging the pieces on the floor, using paper templates, or making a scale diagram.

Several pieces can be brought together to make one statement. For instance, if you are lacking a large piece of art to go over a sofa, you can assemble an arrangement of three pieces to match the shape and size needed.

Here are more grouping tips to consider:

- Leave unfilled areas where the eyes can relax on their journey around the room. If a wall is narrower than three feet wide, leave this space empty.
- To unify multiple pieces of an arrangement, hang them about three to six inches apart, depending on the scale of each piece and the wall space to be filled.
- To achieve balance, align the bottom, side, or top edges of a grouping.
- Keep pairs, sets, and series together on one wall.

Hanging Tips

You've probably heard that art should be mounted at eye level, even though eye level is different for everyone. While this generic advice is somewhat helpful, the best advice here is to remember that we have a tendency to hang items too high on walls. When in doubt, lower is usually better than higher when it comes to wall décor, especially since people spend more time sitting rather than standing in their rooms.

Another guideline for hanging art is to connect it to another piece, since all your client's furniture should already be in place. Hang artwork about six inches above or beside chairs, sofas, end tables, mantles, and plants. Use the top edge of a door frame or the height of a tall cabinet as the elevation cap for mounting your artwork. This will prevent chaotic unevenness around the room and make the wall décor a cohesive part of the room by being an extension of the furnishings.

TIP: Only step or stagger your artwork when the wall space makes the same pattern, such as a staircase wall, lean-to wall, or cathedral shaped wall. Otherwise, hang the pieces side by side or one above the other.

Mirrors

Decorative mirrors should reflect beautiful things, so pay attention to what a mirror will reflect in the room. Try mounting a mirror directly opposite a window to double the room's daylight.

Mounting a mirror above a fireplace typically results in a reflection of the ceiling. Unless the ceiling has been decoratively painted, it's probably not that interesting. If you encounter a built-in mirror above a fireplace, layer items in front of it that are attractive on all sides, such as floral arrangements, statues, topiaries, candlesticks, or wreathes.

You'll need to carry a set of wall hangers and picture hooks to cover all weights and sizes of artwork and mirrors. Other items required for hanging wall décor include a hammer, a tape measure, a stud finder, and a marking pencil. Be sure to have these with you if you're planning to create wall displays.

2.7.3 Window Coverings

In general, the two major families of window coverings are hard and soft. Hard window treatments include blinds, shutters, screens, and specialty glass. Soft window coverings are represented by fabrics used in draperies, curtains, shades, and valances. Depending on the ornamental and practical needs of a room, hard and soft window treatments can be used alone or in combination with each other.

In most cases, window treatments should be kept to a minimum in a staged home. The goal is to allow the most light in during the day, so that heavy drapes or light blocking shades should be packed for the client's move. Light drapes or curtains can also be left in place, but use tie-backs or hold-backs to keep the window space open. Other staging considerations for windows:

- For a room without privacy concerns, you can suggest leaving the windows uncovered.

- For rooms where your clients will need some privacy until the move, use a sheer or lace-like fabric which will allow light to shine through but provide some privacy at night.
- To block an undesirable view and keep the daylight, recommend a window film that looks like stained, frosted, or decorative glass. To see a few options for decorative window films, check out the solutions at Artscape (**http://artscape-inc.com**) and Gila Film Products (**www.gilafilms.com**).

2.7.4 Flooring

Flooring can be one of the biggest challenges to a home staging project's success. Outdated wall-to-wall carpeting, for example, can make a home look badly dated in spite of an otherwise perfect staging design. You may also find that your client's flooring has burn marks or stains, broken tiles, ripped cushion flooring, and so on. All of these can be sticking points for buyers when they're viewing a home and can lower their offers.

You may be tempted to simply cover up a problem by throwing an area rug over a stain in a wooden floor or a few broken tiles. Don't do this. Deliberately hiding damage can result in a backlash from buyers even after they have taken possession of the home. As the home staging professional you may be the one blamed for the defects.

We offered a few tips for masking damage in flooring in section 2.6.2. These are legitimate ways to fix problems with flooring, including replacing broken tiles with matching tiles, fixing holes in carpets with a scrap of leftover carpet of the same color and weave, and so on. However, you may come across problems in flooring that go beyond these quick fixes.

A problem you'll likely come across at some point in your home staging career is outdated carpeting. This can be carpeting of strange colors that aren't commonly seen anymore or weaves that appear dated. Shag carpeting, for example, although once very popular, is not used much today. You may need to convince your client that their shag or bright orange carpeting just doesn't work with your home staging design.

One popular type of flooring today is laminate flooring. It's easy to install and relatively inexpensive. It also comes in a huge variety of colors and materials. In the carpeting examples above, ripping up the old carpets and replacing them with laminate flooring would be a quick and easy solution. Your clients can do the work themselves over a weekend if they're handy, or you can suggest one of your regular contractors (see section 2.11 for information about working with contractors) to do the work for them.

Because flooring is the base for all furniture arrangements to come, you should familiarize yourself with the wide variety of flooring available to homeowners. We'll look briefly here at the various types of flooring so that you can speak with your clients knowledgeably about their flooring options.

Flooring can be classified into either hard or soft categories. Hard flooring includes wood, bamboo, laminate, cement, ceramic tiles, brick, marble, granite, vinyl, linoleum, and slate. These hard surfaces are generally very durable, long lasting, and easy to keep clean. Stained concrete is becoming a popular choice for residential use, although it has been used in commercial and retail spaces for quite awhile.

Bamboo flooring is a great alternative to traditional wood plank flooring because it is harder than oak and is a renewable plant source. Laminate flooring, which simulates wood planks, is also in demand because of its affordability and low maintenance requirements. If your client has beautiful, hard surface floors, you should do your best to highlight this value-added feature.

Soft flooring has a number of cushy benefits such as insulating the floor and improving the acoustics of a room. The two main types of soft flooring are carpets and rugs, which are available in countless colors, designs, and patterns to suit anyone's design style. Also called broadloom, carpets are sold by the yard or as carpet tiles. Carpeting is usually installed wall-to-wall in a room, while rugs are freestanding and moveable.

The fibers used to make carpet and rug yarns are either natural or synthetic in origin. Most modern carpeting is made of synthetic fibers like nylon, olefin, polyester, or acrylic. However, blends of synthetic and natural fibers are often used. For example, wool and nylon are a very durable yet soft duo. Natural fibers include wool, cotton, sisal, and jute, with wool being the most often used. The loops of yarn in a carpet or rug are cut in different lengths or left uncut to create different surface effects like Berber, plush, or sculptured.

2.7.5 Furniture

Once you have worked with the background elements, you can make the room functional and comfortable with the addition of furniture. This is a broad category of items that includes sofas, chairs, chaise lounges, ottomans, tables, chests, cabinets, armoires, beds, and desks.

These furniture pieces can be upholstered in fabric or leather, or they can be made of materials such as wood, metal, wicker, or plastic. You may also encounter built-in wall units and modular pieces. Furniture styles can be modern, contemporary, reproduction, traditional, or antique. Note that in order to be labeled legally as antiques, furnishings have to be at least 100 years old.

When staging a home, it's important to be resourceful and flexible with furniture. Don't limit yourself by the traditional function of a piece, since it could have many alternative uses. A frequently seen example of this is the ottoman. Once just a humble footstool, ottomans are now widely used as coffee tables, extra seating, and window benches.

Likewise, an unused desk tucked away in a study might be the perfect fit as a console table in the client's living room. A shelving unit can be taken off the wall and used as a room divider in a loft apartment. As long as function and safety are considered, you can use furniture pieces in endless ways to enhance your clients' rooms.

Arranging Furniture

First, follow the traffic patterns of the house and pay attention to what you see first as you enter each space. Buyers need to feel welcomed and drawn into the space by what they see at the room's entrance. Then you should consider what changes you will make to each room.

Removing all accessories and nearly all furniture pieces will create a blank canvas for the new room to take shape and make the room's strong or weak points more obvious.

Every space has a focal point of some kind that will be a center of reference for the room's furnishings and accessories, although a few rooms may draw on furniture as the ultimate focal point, such as beds in bedrooms. Look at furniture and accessories as shapes and strategically use them to fill the empty space on floors and walls.

Start with the largest furniture pieces to establish the main seating or furniture area. Balance large or heavy pieces in a room. A large entertainment center can be balanced with a bookcase on the opposite wall. A sofa can be balanced by a similar couch, a loveseat, or two armchairs. Where possible, pull furniture away from the walls and float the arrangement in the central space of the room. Then, fill in with smaller furnishings such as end tables, ottomans, and consoles.

For an illustation of how to use a floating arrangement to highlight the square footage of a room, see the photo below.

The entire square footage of a room can be highlighted by using a floating furniture arrangement. The rug helps to anchor the seating arrangement while the tall tree and large sofa help balance the lofty fireplace mantle.

Conversation areas should be created in almost every room where it makes sense. The living room will have the most need for these areas. Position the main seating group with the focal point and room's architecture in mind. To make the grouping more conducive to comfortable conversation, try a U-shaped or L-shaped furniture layout.

Secondary seating areas are a nice touch if space allows. In a living room corner, two armchairs along with an accent table and lamp make for an inviting reading nook or conversation spot for two. In a bedroom, a chaise lounge or comfy chair is the perfect place to relax anytime of day.

2.7.6 Room Shape

The architecture of a room will help you decide how to successfully place and arrange the furniture and the accessories. The first thing to identify is the room's focal point because this will be the starting point for the furniture placement to begin. It is important to look for the architectural focal point which is the most distinctive part of a room's structure. A room may have multiple focal points, but one should be noticeably dominant. Common focal points you will see include fireplaces, French doors, large picture windows, staircases, built-in bookcases, wall units, or entertainment centers.

Two of the most important architectural features of any room are its shape and its ceilings. It is important to consider how the walls of the room, no matter what its shape, work with the room's ceiling. Ceilings can have a variety of heights and styles and rooms come in a number of different shapes and these components will affect how the space should be laid out. There are several key shapes that describe most rooms: rectangle, square, off-angle, L-shaped, and round.

Rectangle

The rectangular room is probably the most often encountered and tends to have two functions such as a living room and dining room combination. Keep this in mind as you place the furniture to show that the room can have several useful purposes, but always have the main seating area centered on the room's focal point.

Another room shape that falls into the rectangular category is the troublesome oblong room which is commonly compared to a bowling alley lane because it is so long and narrow. Probably the best treatment for an oblong room is to create two or more seating areas and angle them to break up the lengthy thin line of the room. You want the space to be seen as useful and downplay any weak points like being too narrow.

Square

The square room is another commonly encountered shape. Classically, this is a smaller room with one main purpose used, often, as a bedroom or study. The two basic methods for arranging furniture in this kind of space are to place the furnishings at 90-degree or 45-degree angles to the walls. The 45-degree angled layout will create a more casual yet lively look. If the room is a bedroom, the bed, as opposed to an architectural feature, usually ends up being the room's focal point.

Off-angle

A room that fits in the off-angle category is normally a rectangular or square room with one or more corners cut at an angle. Many times, this odd angle is the result of a corner fireplace or a built-in entertainment center. The reliable way to furnish this room is to go with the angle and position the furniture on an angle that matches what the architecture has started.

L-Shaped

The L-shaped room is basically two rectangular rooms overlapping each other at a 90-degree angle and combining into one space shaped like a big L. Similar to rectangular rooms, the L-shaped room typically accommodates two functional areas like a living room and dining room.

The trick here is to unify the two spaces on either side of the L so there is an easy flow around the room's elbow. One technique to try here is placing the furniture in each section of the L on the same angle. This parallel angling will help make the two areas feel more interrelated and accessible to each other.

Round

The round or oval shaped room is not commonly seen, but it is something you may come across one day. Draw an imaginary square inside a round room or an imaginary rectangle inside an oval shaped room—then furnish the room accordingly.

Ceilings

After identifying the room's focal point and taking note of the room's shape, it is now time to analyze how the walls meet up with the ceiling. The reason you should consider this is because the shape of the walls will require precise furniture or accessory arrangements in order to maintain balance with the room's natural architecture.

The line of a room's ceiling can be straight, lean-to, or cathedral shaped. In general, as the ceiling angles up, you want to place taller furniture along the tallest section of the wall. The rest of the wall can then be filled in with shorter objects.

You are open to make high points anywhere along a straight-shaped wall because the line where the ceiling and wall come together is flat and level. For a lean-to or diagonally sloped wall, place taller or heavier furnishings at the tallest point on the wall, and then fill in with shorter pieces on one side. If you encounter a stepped wall, treat it similar to the lean-to wall. For a cathedral or gabled wall shape, place tall furniture under the ceiling's highest point, usually near the middle of the wall, then fill in both sides with smaller furnishings.

Don't forget to improvise! For example, if your client doesn't have an armoire to fill a lofty peak, choose a chest or console table and use art and accessories to extend the visual height of the piece and fill in the vertical space.

Interpreting focal points, room shapes, and wall shapes will translate into the proper placement of furniture and accessories in your client's home. Follow the architecture, and you can't go wrong.

2.7.7 Accessories

Accessories are the details that help characterize a theme or highlight a focal point. They should also harmonize with furnishings and build upon their style or physical shape. Accessories are categorized as functional or decorative, although many times a piece is both. Functional accessories include lamps, clocks, mirrors, books, and screens. Purely decorative accessories include paintings, art prints, sculptures, photographs, and ceramics. A well-balanced room will have a nice mix of both functional and decorative accessories.

During the process of home staging, most small-scale and surplus accessories will be removed from the rooms. This includes personal accessories like family photos. Focus on grouping medium to large-sized pieces that will make a statement without cluttering the rooms. Items can also be gathered into stylish vignettes that add character and tangibility to the room.

Add Decorative Accessories and Lighting

When staging a house, accessories should be kept to a minimum and only used to subtly enhance the space. For redesign services, accessories can be more creatively layered to make dynamic, interesting arrangements. Place lamps in a diagonal or triangular pattern for adequate, balanced lighting all the way through a room.

When arranging items in a bookcase, keep heavier pieces on the lower shelves and use lighter pieces as you go up. Arrange books by size to make graduated patterns. Display some books laying flat with accessories on top.

Rugs can help define a conversation area or other space, but sometimes too many rugs can create clutter or cover attractive flooring that the buyers may want to see. When in doubt, get rid of the rugs.

The kitchen, living room, and master bedroom are prime areas that capture the attention of potential buyers, and the state of these rooms may well influence their decision to buy or to keep looking. Even if the rest of a house is vacant, these areas should be staged to showcase their function and beauty.

For a more pulled together and interesting space in your client's home, the major surfaces should be decorated using the homeowner's accessories along with your own props. Creating vignettes in key areas of a staged home can make open houses and realtor showings even more memorable to buyers.

As mentioned a few pages ago, a vignette is an ensemble of accessories that highlight a room's function or decorative details. When building vignettes for both staging and redesign projects, there are basic guidelines to help your arrangements come together:

- Group objects by similar shapes, colors, themes, or other shared attributes.
- Cluster items in odd numbered groupings.
- Keep pairs and sets of items together and display them near each other.
- Build symmetrical or asymmetrical pyramid shapes with your accessories. A tall or large object will be the peak of your pyramid, while smaller items will fill in the body and base of the pyramidal shape.

2.8 Staging Vacant Homes

You won't always be staging houses in which the client is still residing until the sale happens; sometimes you will be staging vacant homes. After all, empty houses probably need staging the most in order to bring some life and energy into the space. There are special considerations for this type of staging project.

Since the kitchen, living room, and master bedroom are areas that buyers use most to make their purchase decision, the feeling of these key rooms will sway their choice either to buy the house or to continue searching. Even if the remainder of the residence is left unadorned, these areas should be staged to showcase their purpose and best features.

Vignettes

Vignettes are one way to dress up each room without furnishing the entire house. A vignette is an ensemble of accessories that highlight a room's function or decorative details. Like creating tablescape designs, vignettes can be built on any horizontal surface including countertops, dressers, bathroom vanities, mantles, window seats, and bookshelves. Cluster items in sets of three, five, or other odd numbered groupings.

The basic technique to creating a vignette starts with selecting a large piece like a vase or lamp. Then fill in with objects of various heights to form a rough pyramid shape around the main item. The large object is the peak of your pyramid, and the other items form the body and base of the pyramid shape.

Here are several tips for creating vignettes:

- *Kitchen Island:* An inviting vignette on a kitchen island might include: a basket filled with baguettes, a bottle of wine or sparkling mineral water, two glasses, a set of crystal candlesticks with ivory tapers, and a wedge of cheese under glass.
- *Living Room:* Dress up a living room with a mantle vignette featuring a large attractive painting, a few books, weighty bookends, large candlesticks, and a decorative clock. A more in-depth vignette would include an armchair with a side table, lamp, and table top accessories. Drape a throw across the chair with an open book laid on the seat.
- *Master Bedroom:* In a master bedroom, an inflatable raised air mattress can be dressed as a hotel style bed with tailored sheets and pillows. A pleasant bedside table vignette might include: a lamp, roses or orchids, massage oils, a bottle of sparkling mineral water, and two glasses. As well, the master bath can host a small vignette of bath salts, candles, flowers, and loofah sponges on a silver tray.

The color section in this book further illustrates how to effectively use a vignette in a home that you are staging.

Other Options

To fully furnish a vacant house, you can arrange for furniture rentals through local dealers offering these services. There are several benefits to using a rental company: they deliver and pick-up the items, they maintain the furnishings, and you can select from a wide variety of in-stock choices.

Another option for furnishing a whole house is to keep your own inventory of furniture in a storage facility. Upsides to this are that you own the pieces, you can access the furniture on your schedule, and you will probably save money in the long run. The downsides are the initial investment in the inventory, the storage fees, and transporting the furniture back and forth. The furnishings will also need to be kept looking fresh and clean for the best presentation.

Jason Maxwell of Equity Enhancers Home Staging knows firsthand the challenges of staging vacant homes:

> "When entering the home staging business… I found that my biggest struggle was figuring out how to service the vacant home market. While there are many owner-occupied homes that need to be staged, there is a huge need in the market for vacant homes. The challenge was capturing that market while maintaining a profit. After having searched many furniture rental companies… I realized it would be up to me to purchase my own inventory if I wanted to fulfill the needs of my clients at a reasonable price. Now I have the ability to furnish 30-plus vacant homes ranging from $60,000 to $2,000,000."

An additional source of income for home stagers is furnishing vacant properties with pieces available for sale to those who tour or buy the home. For example, builders' model homes are sometimes staged with furniture or art that is also for sale. This type of arrangement may not be welcome by all clients or realtors, so be sure to present the idea as an option, not a requirement. The overall goal is to sell the house, not your wares; this is just a bonus opportunity when appropriate. The realtor can inform those who view the home that the furnishings are for sale through your home staging company. Discreet price tags can be placed under a couch cushion or on the back of an art frame.

2.9 Creating Curb Appeal: Yards and Exterior

The exterior of a client's residence can actually be more significant than the interior. This is because a buyer who is not impressed with a home's outer appearance may never see the beautifully staged rooms inside.

For that reason, staging is vitally important for the outside areas of a house.

As part of staging a client's interior space, you will also be making exterior recommendations and helping your clients add curb appeal. Staging outdoor areas will help lure buyers out of their cars and onto your client's property. If your clients need help preparing these spaces, be ready to jump in with your own services, those of a subcontractor, or refer a company. Here are some curb appeal ideas for you or your client to consider:

2.8.1 Yard Work

De-cluttering and cleaning the front, back, and side yards of a house is the first step. Items that are considered outdoor clutter when selling a house should be packed up, stored, or donated to charity. This includes grilling equipment, empty flower pots, lumber, kid's toys, holiday lighting, sports equipment, gardening materials, and tools. Your client's lawn and patios will appear larger and be more appealing without all these untidy bits and pieces.

Trees, shrubs, and flowerbeds should be in peak condition. If something is dead, remove it from the yard. Trees and shrubs should be trimmed or cut so that the house is plainly visible and not hidden behind overgrown foliage. Too much of anything can be a bad thing! Trimming will also let more light into your client's windows for brighter rooms and keep tree branches from resting on rooftops. Flowerbeds should be cleared of small ornaments, weeds, overgrowth, and dead plants. Healthy, colorful vegetation ought to be planted and finished off with mulch or other attractive ground cover.

Lawns or grassy areas should be kept mowed, watered, and weed-free. Also, a client's lawn will look ten times better if it is edged. If needed, they can apply a quick greening fertilizer with the capability to make lawns greener in a week or less. If the lawn is beyond saving, the client ought to consider laying new sod or having new grass seeds applied by a hydromulch or hydroseed process. Fences around these grassy areas should be mended and perhaps stained or painted if the wood is faded.

2.9.2 House Exterior

Freshening up the painted surfaces on the outside of a client's house is an inexpensive way to make a real difference. In addition to trim, siding, and gutter repainting, the garage door and front door can be greatly improved with a little paint. Remind your clients to keep overall paint choices neutral to appeal to the widest range of potential buyers. If a little color is desired, the front door is a spot where black, red, and another dramatic color can be attempted. For a more interesting look on a wood-tone door, have the client apply a rich stain color.

Roofs, and any attached gutters, should be clean and in superior condition. Missing or loose shingles should be replaced, and any gutter leaks must be patched up.

Cleaning and polishing a home's windows will make the exterior really shine and will boost the daylight level of your client's home for a brighter showing house. Any broken windowpanes or cracked glass must be fixed.

Encourage your clients to look for insect issues early in the staging process so they have time to combat any problems such as ants, wasps, bees, or termites. Not only are these pests destructive to yards and homes, but a number of people are highly allergic to certain insects. To ensure the comfort of buyers, get rid of the bugs.

Nice additions that can add to curb appeal include containers filled with healthy flowers, shutters, arbors, fountains, and window boxes. As with all staging, items should be kept to a minimum so that it enhances the exterior and allows the house to be seen clearly by buyers.

2.9.3 Additional Exterior Considerations

Driveways, Walks, and Patios

Driveways and sidewalks that have cracks or stains should be patched up and cleaned to look their best since they tend to take up a lot of visual area in the front of a house. Power washing uses a high-pressure water sprayer to quickly improve the appearance of solid surfaces, and these units can usually be rented at a large hardware store. Gravel surfaces may also need attention in the form of new rocks or a thorough cleaning of the existing rocks.

Patios and decks can also benefit from power washing and a coat of sealant or stain to freshen them up. Plus, you can stage these areas with an inviting outdoor seating arrangement which adds square footage to your client's house.

Neighboring Homes

A client who has an unkempt home neighboring them will definitely appreciate any suggestions you may have to help remedy the problem.

As an unbiased third party, you can attempt a casual chat with the neighbor explaining that the house is being staged to sell. Most likely, the neighbor will respond with a little understanding and then proceed to clean up their property to some extent (some will do more than others). This technique is least likely to upset neighborly relations because you are an intermediary in the process.

When all else fails, recommend a screen of shrubs be planted or a trellis screen be erected in strategic spots to reduce the undesirable view.

2.10 Creating Ambience

While a staged house is open to the buying public, all the preparations come down to the last few details—the ambience inside the house. Ambience is the atmosphere, mood, or feeling that is generated by the environment of a staged house. Your client has cleared the clutter, the house is squeaky clean, and you've beautifully staged the furniture and accessories. Now all that's left is to add that final layer of ambience.

Here are some ideas to offer your clients for their open house day or when the house is being shown:

- *Give buyers a sense of ease:* As their real estate agent will probably also recommend, your clients should not be in the house when buyers are touring it. This will allow buyers to freely explore the rooms and express concerns to the realtor. The homeowner can wait in close proximity by visiting a neighbor or going for a stroll around the block.

- *Remove personal items:* As mentioned, you should recommend that your clients put away any daily necessities that remain in the staged home: store medications and toiletries in a cabinet, take out the garbage daily to prevent odors, keep trash cans out of sight, close toilet seats and lids, and lower garage doors.
- *Maintain a comfortable house temperature:* Have your clients keep the house at a comfortable temperature at all times, because a buyer could pop by anytime while the house is on the market.
- *Play soft music:* Another nice touch is for your clients to play soft, low-volume music throughout their house. They should select a radio station featuring smooth jazz, easy listening music, soft pop, soft rock, or classical music.

2.10.1 Lighting

Buyers respond nicely to a well-lit, radiant house. When staging a home, an abundance of natural and artificial light will be necessary for properly showing the residence.

Any lighting that is not directly from the sun is considered artificial. Since natural lighting is always preferred to artificial sources, start by letting in more sunlight. Before each showing, have your client open or tie back all the blinds, shades, and drapes to promote a fresh, airy feeling in the house.

To help fill the rooms with even more luminosity, your clients should also use every single one of their lamps and lighting fixtures during the showings. If they won't be home during the showing hours, they can set up timers that keep lights on during the peak times of 9:00 a.m. and 6:00 p.m. Even during the day, a home's lights should be burning brightly, so buyers aren't walking into dimly-lit rooms.

TIP: A candle warmer is an alternative to lit candles, which can pose a fire risk if left unattended. This nifty device is very similar to a coffee mug warmer and heats up glass jarred candles safely and discreetly.

2.10.2 Smells

There's room for only enjoyable smells in a staged home, so get rid of any unpleasant or uncomfortable odors in your client's house. Instead of just trying to cover up the smell, you should locate the cause of the offending odor. Bad smells can emanate from food preparation, pets, mildew, smoking, and many other culprits.

Here are some tips:

- Circulate air through a client's house by opening the windows and using fans. Tough areas may require a window to stay cracked at all times and the addition of an air purifying device.
- You might suggest that a client have their air ducts professionally cleaned if there is a dusty, moldy smell throughout the home. Carpets or rugs can also be freshened up with a professional cleaning.
- For pet-related odors, apply a bacterial or enzyme digester to any stains or stinky areas.
- Suggest that your clients take out the garbage daily to prevent unwanted smells.
- If your client's garage has any strong odors from oil, gasoline, or pesticides, remove those substances. For oil stains on concrete, they should first apply sawdust, cornmeal, or kitty litter to soak up excess oil. After leaving this absorbent material on for about a day, they should sweep it into the trash before power-washing the floor using a high-pressure water sprayer and a degreaser.

Toni Bouman, owner of Toni B Interiors and a stager with almost twenty-five years experience in real estate, offers her tips for adding irresistible aromas to a staged property. She recommends using "a candle warmer that stays on all the time with a vanilla candle… and baking cookies or bread at open houses." This evokes fond memories and warm feelings in the people who tour the house, although they may not even realize why.

2.11 Working with Contractors

In the process of staging a home, there will be a multitude of tasks that you can either tackle yourself or hire other people to do. The decision should be based on your personal limitations and your available time to complete the odd jobs. For some items, you will want to arrange for subcontractors who are experts in their chosen fields. After all, you may not have the time or the inclination to be a jack of all trades.

During a client consultation, you may suggest that they add window treatments, add a few new furniture pieces, or repaint a few rooms. Your proposal (discussed in section 2.3) should outline your company's costs to provide these services. Homeowners who have a tight budget may opt to implement your recommendations on their own. If a client wants to pay your company to do the work, you can complete some or all of the tasks yourself.

2.11.1 Types of Contractors

One of the keys to success as a home stager is to find great people with whom to align yourself. The most important requirement for your subcontractors is that they are appropriately insured, bonded, and/or licensed to offer their services. Get a copy of their insurance policy or the number of their license to keep on file.

The typical subcontractors that you may end up hiring for home staging projects include:

- Carpet and air duct cleaners
- Drapery workrooms
- Electricians
- Flooring installers
- Handyman services
- House cleaners and maids
- Landscapers and lawn services
- Moving services for furniture and storage

- Painters and faux finishers
- Plumbers
- Professional organizers
- Repair services
- Upholsterers
- Wallpaper installers
- Window treatment/blinds installers

2.11.2 How to Find Contractors

Start by asking your family and friends about their referrals for trustworthy service professionals. Also, ask other service providers that you're already working with for their recommendations—they are wonderful sources of insider information.

Some of the industry associations listed in section 3.3.3 have directories of contractors available to members. Consider joining one of these associations to help you network with other home stagers and ask their advice about choosing the right contractors.

While websites, magazines, and national directories can be excellent sources for contractors, don't neglect the local market. You'll want to consider going local on most services including painting services, equipment rentals, and repair work. In addition to the Yellow Pages and online searches, you may be able to find local suppliers and contractors through your Chamber of Commerce. Many Chambers publish a membership directory listing companies by category with company contact information.

Whether you get a potential subcontractor's name from a trusted resource or from the phone book, you should request three references and their commercial price list. In the client's eyes, a subcontractor's behavior and customer service reflects back on you. Don't put up with poor-quality work or bad attitudes, as there are scores of good service people just waiting for your call.

Here are a few examples of resources that can help you find contractors for your business:

- *American Society of Interior Designers Industry Partner Directory*
https://member.asid.org/asidssa/asidmemssaipdir.query_page

- *Interior Design Magazine Buyers Guide*
http://resourceguide.interiordesign.net

- *e-renovate (Canada)*
www.erenovate.com/local-contractors.php

2.11.3 Choosing Contractors

When you hire or recommend contractors to a client, you are ultimately responsible for how well these contractors do their jobs, so you will need to find businesses you can depend on to do the job right, by the agreed-upon deadline, for the agreed-upon price. Remember your name is on the line if you bring in a contractor and they don't come through in a timely or professional manner or within cost. So look for someone reliable, and have at least one back-up for each job.

Once you have completed a number of staging projects for clients, you will know which contractors deliver what they promise, and you will have built a preferred list of contractors you can recommend. Until then, you will need to check out your contractors closely in order to recommend them to clients.

To help you choose contractors, make appointments to meet either by phone or in person. Ask what services they provide, their rates, and their availability. You need to know that you can depend on them, and that they will be willing to work overtime if necessary to keep their agreements with you. (Unfortunately, some busy companies consider deadlines to be "suggestions" rather than requirements.)

Before working with a contractor, you should do an online search to see if there are any complaints about them. You can also try checking companies with the Better Business Bureau (BBB) at **www.bbb.org**, but keep in mind that the BBB is not a government agency. It is a private organization that makes money from fees paid by many of the companies the BBB rates and, as an article by Leslie M. Marable in *Money* magazine reported, BBBs "sometimes fail to give unsatisfactory ratings to companies plagued by a history of serious complaints."

You should definitely ask the contractor for references from previous clients. Call those references to find out what services the company provided, and whether the clients were satisfied. To uncover any problems, ask the client what they would do differently if they were hiring the same contractor, and which parts of the services they were least satisfied with. Also check if the contractor holds liability insurance, which may protect both them and you if the work is not satisfactory.

If you choose a contractor for a specific client or project, get agreements (e.g. for costs, delivery dates, services to be provided) in writing. With some contractors, a contract is critical. This is your insurance policy that the contractor will provide what you've agreed to. Most suppliers are comfortable working with contracts, and will probably be able to provide this document for you. If they do not have a contract, you can ask them to sign a confirmation letter (like the one below) and return it to you.

Sample Contractor Confirmation Letter

P2 Painters
123 Anywhere Road
Anytown, USA

Re: Smith Home Staging Project– June 20

Dear Paul Painter,

I am writing you today to confirm the painting arrangements for the Smith home staging project, which is to take place June 21. As the home stager for Mr. and Mrs. Smith, I will be responsible for co-ordination of your services and will now be the contact person on any matters relating to the painting job. My understanding of the arrangements is as follows:

- The colors chosen are Midnight Mist and Seashell Blue, to be picked up by you at Anytown Paint Supply, as agreed in our meeting on Thursday, June 12.
- The room to be painted will be cleared of furniture and painting is to commence by 9:00 a.m.

- The clients will be at the house to let you and your crew into the residence.

My clients (Mr. and Mrs. Smith) are responsible for payment to you for all services rendered including deposits and for any charges for cancellation of your service. I will contact you several days before June 21 to ensure everything is in place and on schedule.

We look forward to working with you, and I know the Smiths will be delighted with their new colors. Please do not hesitate to call me at 888-555-1212 or email me at lola@lolastager.net if you have any further questions.

Please sign this letter and return one copy to my attention at:

Lola Stager
Home Staging by Lola
255 Willow Tree Lane
Anytown, USA

Sincerely,

Lola Stager

The parties hereto agree with the contents contained herein and acknowledge receipt of this letter.

________________________	________________________
Paul Painter	Lola Stager
Owner	Home Staging by Lola
P2 Painters	

For certain types of projects that cannot be easily covered with a flat fee, you can allow a subcontractor to visit the client's house and then provide you with an informed bid. This process will help you uncover any issues that you may not have recognized on your own, so that you do not underbid or overbid a client.

If the contractor provides you with a contract, review it carefully before signing, and make sure all key points are covered. Some of the critical information that must be spelled out includes:

- Exactly what the contractor will (and will not) provide, e.g. if the contractor is a drapery workroom, will they provide measuring and installation services.
- Exact times for when they are available to perform the services.
- Any additional requirements that you must provide.
- Detailed payment schedule, including deposits and when payment is due in full.
- Cancellation policy, including any fees payable if the product or service ordered is cancelled.

Remember, contracts are negotiable. If there is anything in the contract that you don't like, or anything you don't fully understand, discuss it before signing. Once that document is signed, you will have little recourse if something goes awry.

TIP: Unless you will be paying the contractor yourself, make sure the contract is between the contractor and your client, not between the contractor and you. If you enter into a contract with a contractor, you will be held personally liable for payment if the work is cancelled or postponed.

2.11.4 Financial Arrangements

You have several options for your financial arrangements with clients when purchasing any services needed for your home staging projects.

Purchasing Services for Your Clients

If you are purchasing services for your client, one option is to pay the contractor, then submit the invoice to your client along with other agreed upon expenses. In this case, you would need to specify in your client contract that this service will be billed in addition to your fee. To avoid being out of pocket, you can ask your client for a deposit or an advance on your fees.

Another option may be to have the contractor bill your client directly. That way you won't risk being in the position where you have to pay the contractor's bill before you have been paid by the client. However, this may create additional administrative work for both the contractor and your client, and you may prefer not to have the client establish a relationship directly with your supplier.

> **TIP:** It is not unheard of for a client to drop a home stager they perceive as the "middle man" and deal directly with contractors on future projects. Unless you absolutely trust your contractor not to compete for business with you, you may not want to take that risk.

Another option is to offer the contractor's services under the umbrella of your company. In that case the contractor is working for you rather than your client and would invoice your company. You in turn would invoice the client for the service as part of your fee. Although you might be out of pocket for a while until you are paid by the client, this option may ultimately be more profitable for you.

When giving the client a quote for your services, you could include the contractor's services at a price marked up to cover your overhead. For example, if the contractor charges you $200, you might charge the client a fee of $300 for that particular service. Another option, instead of charging the client more for the contractor's service, is to charge the contractor a commission, such as 25 percent of the cost of the services. That way the client won't pay any more than if they went directly to the contractor for the service.

If you decide to work with contractors in this way, you should make sure you have a written agreement in place. The agreement should outline exactly what services the contractor will provide, the date the services will be provided by, and what the exact cost will be. In section 2.3.5 you will find a sample letter of agreement and a more detailed services contract which you can adapt to use with service providers. Remember to have your lawyer review any agreement to ensure it meets your needs.

Paying Contractors

Many contractors will expect to be paid at the time they supply the product or service. However, in some cases, they might expect a deposit or full payment before delivery of the goods or services. For example, if you order custom draperies, you will need to make a deposit before the work is undertaken and pay in full when they are completed.

You may choose to pay all costs upfront and then invoice the client. However, to avoid risking your own funds, you have a couple of options. One option, if you are purchasing for a client that you know has good credit, is to have the contractor carry out the service and invoice the client directly. (Make sure you arrange this in advance with the client, so the invoice will be paid by them.) Another option is to get a check from your client so you can pay the vendor when you pick up products or book services.

After you have finished the job and the subcontractor has been paid, it's a good idea to summarize the experience you had with that particular contractor. If you keep a record of how the contractor performed, what services they provided, and the cost of the services, you will readily know which contractors did a good job and for a reasonable price and know who to choose or refer for future projects.

A sample Subcontractor Job Summary Sheet appears on the next page.

2.11.5 Referrals

Referring Clients to Contractors

In some cases, you may recommend that your client buy a product or service from a particular business, and your client will make the purchase alone. For example, you might recommend that your client buy window coverings from XYZ Windows. In this case, you may recommend XYZ simply because you believe they will provide the best products for your client's needs. You won't get anything in return for your recommendation from XYZ.

However, if there are companies you believe provide excellent products and services that you plan to recommend to your clients, why not ask them to provide you with something in return for referring them to your clients? You might simply agree informally to refer clients to each other's business which may result in some additional business for your company.

Sample Subcontractor Job Summary Sheet

[Your Company Name]

Date: ______________________________

Client Name: ______________________________

Address: ______________________________

____

____

City, St, Zip: ______________________________

Phone: ______________________________

Sub Name: ______________________________

Description of Services Performed *[note any issues that came up and how they were handled]*:

Did client make payment? ❑ Yes ❑ No

Date: ______________

Amount of Invoice: $______________ *[attach copy of invoice]*

Referral Fees and Commissions

An increasingly common practice in business is the payment of "referral fees." For example, if you refer a client to an electrician or a professional organizer, that contractor pays you a fee as a thank you for referring business to them that they otherwise would not have. Likewise, you could pay them a referral fee for any staging business they send your way.

There are no firm guidelines for the amount of a referral fee. It can be whatever you negotiate with a particular contractor, and might be a percentage of what they earn from the referral (e.g. five to 20 percent of the amount of the client's first purchase from the contractor) or a flat fee. In some cases, a contractor will not be willing to pay a referral fee (for example, if they are already booked up with work at their full fee).

Work out a referral plan with these businesses so that any clients you send their way will result in a referral fee or commission for you. This can be a flat rate, like $25 per referral, or a percentage rate such as 10% of all sales generated by the referred client. The referral rate to be negotiated will depend on the overall cost of the service. Lower cost service providers, like house cleaners, won't be able to offer as large a referral fee as a higher cost service provider can, such as a landscaper or painter.

You may also be able to work out a special rate for your clients in addition to your referral fee. For example, let's say a carpet cleaner will offer a special discount rate for your referred clients plus pay you a referral fee. The carpet cleaner could provide you with custom coupons or cards featuring the special discount. Your client is more likely to go with your referral because you've researched to find the best service provider, and their service is discounted off the regular price.

3. Developing Your Skills and Knowledge

Now that you know the tasks involved in home staging, you should ensure that your knowledge and training is up to the challenge. The public is more informed than ever before about home staging from popular TV shows such as *Designed to Sell* on HGTV and *Sell This House* on A&E. However, clients will be turning to you as the expert. By developing your home staging skills and knowledge, you can boost your self-confidence and increase your clients' confidence in your expertise. This chapter describes essential skills and knowledge needed by home stagers, and ways you can acquire and develop those abilities.

3.1 Skills and Knowledge You Will Need

3.1.1 Knowledge of Interior Decorating

Having a knack for good design may seem like an instinctive quality that certain people are just born knowing. While many people who are attracted to a career in home staging do have great taste and artistic tendencies from an early age, interior decorating skills can be learned. In the beginning stages of your career, you can compensate for a lack of experience with training and education on design elements, principles, and methods. Continuing this pursuit of knowledge as you build your business will make you more adept as a home stager.

Luckily, the emphasis of home staging is to create a pleasing backdrop for the buyer's imagination—not something that requires award-winning interior decorating. However, having a firm grasp of basic design principles will make your job a lot easier when you are staring at a client's blank wall or a chaotic room full of furniture and accessories.

The next few pages provide a basic overview of interior design elements, principles, and theories. Later in this chapter you will find a variety of resources and ideas that can help you quickly develop your interior decorating knowledge. Combined with the techniques you learned for assessing interior spaces in the previous chapter, you'll soon be able to put theory into practice and make your decorating ideas a success.

Design Elements

In order for anyone to effectively design a home space, they must first understand and know how to successfully implement the elements of design. In this section, we'll look at some basic elements of design that you might want to learn more about. (We'll tell you how to learn more later in this chapter.)

The basic interior design elements include:

Color

The use of color can influence many things in a room including mood, shapes, and sizes. One of the most important things for a home stager to know about color is "temperature" which indicates whether a color is warm or cool. Warm colors (reds and oranges) are considered to be "advancing" because they seem as though they are coming closer to the viewer which can make a space feel cozy. Cool colors (greens and blues) are called "receding" colors and can make a room seem more spacious. You can find additional valuable information about color theory online at a site such as Pittsburgh Paint's Voice of Color website at **www.voiceofcolor.com/en/aboutcolor/color_theory**.

To assist you in finding colors that work together, you can purchase a color wheel online for as little as $10 from The Color Wheel Company (**www.colorwheelco.com**). Following are the basic colors you'll be working with:

- *Primary colors:* Red, yellow, and blue.
- *Secondary colors:* Primary colors combined in pairs to make orange, green, and purple.
- *Tertiary colors (also known as intermediate colors):* An equal combination of a primary color and a secondary color next to it on the color wheel. The six tertiary colors are: blue-purple, blue-green, yellow-green, yellow-orange, red-orange, and red-purple.
- *Neutral:* Colors that aren't on the color wheel. The true neutral colors are black, white, and grey. Other colors, such as silver and brown, may also be used as neutral colors in decorating.

The base color schemes include:

- *Achromatic:* A striking application of black, white, or a range of grays.
- *Monotone:* Uses neutralized colors that are in between warm and cool such as beige, tan, off-white, cream, brown, and brown-black.
- *Monochromatic:* Utilizes one color in a mixture of tints, tones, and shades to create a unified feeling.
- *Analogous:* Makes use of three or more color segments which are beside each other on the color wheel. For example, if you use red, red-orange, and red-violet this works as an analogous color scheme because these colors are next to each other and red is a base color of both orange and violet.
- *Complementary:* A contrasting color scheme that uses both cool and warm colors that are across from each other on the color wheel. Red-green, blue-orange, and yellow-purple are direct complements. There are also split complements and triads that use three colors. Double complements and tetrad color schemes use four contrasting colors.

Lighting

Lighting allows the elements of a room to be seen and can affect mood, colors, and comfort. A room's lighting elements are very important to the overall function and feeling of the space. Artificial lighting falls into three general categories:

- *General or ambient:* Typically produced by ceiling fixtures such as chandeliers or recessed lights that light up most of a room. Torchieres and floor lamps can also provide ambient lighting.
- *Task or local:* These fixtures provide focused light for reading, working, or any other task. Examples include table lamps, track lighting, and under-the-cabinet lighting for the kitchen.
- *Accent:* Mostly just for aesthetics and drama, accent lighting is a targeted light that shines on an object or specific area. Accent lights include up lights and small spotlights that draw attention to artwork, sculptures, or plants.

Line

Line affects the perceived size of an object or a room, and gives space a sense of direction. Types of lines include:

- Horizontal lines, such as shelves or a bed, enhance the feeling of relaxation and strength in a room.
- Vertical lines, found in, for example, long draperies, augment the height and stateliness of a room.
- Diagonal lines, such as a diagonally patterned fabric, create movement within a space.
- Curved lines, like those of round tables, lend a graceful, feminine element to a room.
- Straight lines, like doors, chair molding, and square tables, are more masculine and impart a feeling of strength.

Mass

Mass is a three-dimensional shape that has volume. In any room, mass is represented by objects like furniture and accessories. Simple mass forms include rectangles, squares, triangles, diamonds, spheres, and circles.

Pattern

Patterns are repeated colors, lines or textures. As we look around a room, our eyes distinguish patterns formed by the architecture, the furniture, and the decorative motifs found on objects in the space. Your eye wants to find patterns in a room's arrangements and accessories. The fabric patterns that are selected for a room will have an impact on the feel of the room. For example:

- Patterns with geometric shapes will give the room a contemporary look.
- Patterns with checks will give the room a casual look.
- Patterns with tapestries or paisleys will give the room a more formal look.
- Fabrics with a light airy pattern such as florals will give a room a more airy, open and casual look.
- Some patterns (such as stripes) can give either a formal or casual look depending on the type of fabric used.

Shape

Shape is the contour or outline of an object, which is visible as curved or straight lines. Most shapes in architecture and interiors are rectangles and squares because of their versatility, stability, and efficient use of space. Effectively introducing diagonal and curved forms into a rectangular or square space is one of the challenges of how to design great rooms. (Room shapes are discussed in detail in section 2.7.6.)

Space

Every room or enclosed area contains space. The elements of design work in unison to fill the positive and negative areas of all spaces. In a living room for example, furniture is a positive use of space while walking paths through the room are a negative use of space. Proper use of space (for example, positioning furniture correctly) can make a room appear more functional.

Texture

When we touch the surface of objects, we experience texture. The basic types of texture are glossy or dull, soft or firm, and smooth or rough, and can be found in flooring, area rugs, walls, fabrics, draperies, furnishings, etc. Texture can be either tactile (e.g., the feel of leather, silk, burlap, velvet, and chenille) or visual (smooth or satiny looking fabrics, or rough or coarse looking fabrics).

Different textures have different durability. Smooth or shiny surfaces may show scratches and fingerprints easily. Rougher surfaces may be more resilient, but they can be harder to keep clean. Glossy paint is easy to clean but can emphasize wall blemishes. Flat or dull paint helps conceal defects on wall surfaces, but does not stand up well to cleanings.

Design Principles

Closely related to the elements of design, the principles of design are another building block of great rooms. These principles have developed over time with the study of nature and the fine arts. The elements of design mentioned above can be used to realize these basic principles of design:

Balance

Balance is harmonious order created in a room by arranging all the elements of design into a whole. When our eyes identify the weight of items in a room, we get a sense of balance or imbalance based on the visual lightness or heaviness of objects and features. Colors, textures, patterns and objects are all part of the balance equation.

Types of balance include:

- Symmetrical balance is when two matching items are positioned equally along a line. For example, a set of two sconces each placed exactly one foot away on either side of a painting creates linear symmetry. Symmetry is used mostly in formal traditional interiors, but can be boring if used to a great extent.
- Asymmetrical balance uses items of assorted shapes, sizes, and colors to create a sense of equality. Some asymmetrical balance makes a room more visually interesting than one that is complete-

ly symmetrical. For instance, a sofa can be asymmetrically balanced by two smaller armchairs, or a large vase can be balanced by a trio of candlesticks on a fireplace mantle.

- Radial balance is experienced, for example, when viewing a large chandelier or chairs encircling a round table. The circular arrangement creates a design balance that radiates from a central point; in this case, the table.

Emphasis

Every room should have an emphasis, which is a focal point or noticeable center of attention. This emphasis is crucial to providing a sense of ease because your eyes naturally look for this visual anchor when viewing a room. Maybe the room has a fireplace, a great view, or a dramatic piece of furniture—any of these elements can be the emphasis of a room. Color can help when attention needs to be brought to a focal point such as placing a vibrant painting above a fireplace.

Harmony

Harmony is a unifying theme. However, the room design should have just the right amount of variety to add interest. The easiest way to do this is to feature one main design style to bring a space together, but incorporate a few unexpected or interesting items.

Rhythm

Rhythm in interiors is continuity that helps the eye flow easily around a room. This can be achieved through:

- Gradation creates rhythm by arranging items by size: This may be seen in items like a kitchen canister set that is arranged from big to small or in a set of nesting tables.

- Repetition helps create rhythm when a pattern, color, or other design element is repeated. Using the same fabric on a chair, sofa pillows, and a drapery is a common way to use rhythm. Remember, too much of anything can be a bad thing, so don't overuse any one element.

- Transition instills rhythm with the use of curved lines that soften hard edges. For example, a round table will help take the edge off a room's corner, helping your eyes comfortably continue around the room. Arched windows and the swags in a drape are also examples of transitional rhythm.

Scale and Proportion

The perceptible size of different items in a room. Scale usually references the human body as a starting point. As an example, furniture for children is considered a scaled down version of furniture for adults. Proportion may refer to the size of an item relative to other items in the room.

To show how scale and proportion work together, consider a lamp. The lamp's base and the lampshade should be proportionate to each other, but the lamp must be the right scale for the table on which it is placed, not too big or too small.

The photo below illustrates scale and proportion:

The sofa in this modern living room is nicely proportioned to the scale of the room. The seating has been oriented towards the large patio window which is the main focal point of the room. The armoire has been strategically placed to extend the window area and to complement the ceiling angles.

Design Theories

Most homes can be staged using one of the following basic design theories, with alterations made along the way for special situations. When thinking about the arrangement of furniture and accessories, you can employ one or more of the following design theories to meet your client's needs.

Feng Shui

Feng shui, pronounced "fung shway," is a practice of achieving harmony and stability in a space and is becoming very popular among the general population. This art of thoughtfully positioning objects was developed in ancient China and translates loosely as "wind and water." The central theory of feng shui contends that all items and spaces are made of different energies which have an effect on each other. Practitioners of this theory combine the five elements of water, fire, earth, wood, and metal, along with a balance of yin and yang (passive and active energy).

When decorating interiors, the items brought into each space are believed to have positive and negative effects on a home's energy. Balancing these energies is the art of feng shui which is intended to align physical surroundings with a person's hopes or goals. Some of the basic feng shui design principles call for clearing out clutter, arranging furniture in comfortable ways, and carefully choosing color palettes. For example, orienting furniture so that occupants can see the room's entrance will promote a sense of security. Also, the energy in a hallway can be slowed down by hanging artwork or interesting items along the walls.

Put another way, an interior space is a reflection of a person's life or mental state. A cluttered home can be an expression of the struggles in that individual's reality. When buyers enter a cluttered home or a home with bad energy, they probably won't stay long or make an offer on the property. That's why home staging is so valuable when selling a house and why redesigns are able to put clients at ease in their homes.

A couple of good resources for more information include the World of Feng Shui website at **www.wofs.com** and Feng Shui Directory at **www.fengshuidirectory.com**.

Gestalt

Another way to think about space and objects is from a spatial mind-set such as Gestalt psychology. Princeton University's WordNet defines gestalt as "a configuration or pattern of elements so unified as a whole that it cannot be described merely as a sum of its parts." Gestalt roughly translates from German as "shape" or "form." Gestalt theory explores how the human brain arranges objects into straightforward patterns and explains why objects clustered by proximity or by similar features create satisfying groupings.

For instance, a large rectangular living room is a shape that can be divided into smaller sections. This allows for two functional areas to be established such as a main seating area and a dining area. Within these spaces, each piece of furniture can be viewed as a distinct shape or form that is used to fill the space appropriately. Follow this all the way down to the accessories which are forms that should be grouped by similarities in color, theme, material, or shape. This simplification and organization of complex objects is well received by the brain, creating a sense of harmony for the viewer. If you are using a camel-back sofa as the main piece of furniture in a room, pair it with a round coffee table or curvy end tables. Repetition of furniture shapes and fabric patterns will lead to a cohesive room design.

Greek Geometry

Lastly, we must not forget the ancient Greeks, who were avid students of scale and proportion. Their efforts resulted in the golden rectangle, the golden section, and the golden mean, which are often incorporated into architecture and interiors. As well, the ancient Greeks found that groupings of odd numbers were more enjoyable than even- numbered groups.

The golden rectangle sets up the most pleasing width to length ratio for room shapes as 2:3. A room that is eight feet wide by twelve feet long will be easier to work with and more pleasing than a room that is ten by ten. For example, a square living room can be made cozier with an L-shaped or U-shaped rectangular furniture arrangement. In addition, furnishings are often rectangular in form—sofas, dining tables, rugs, artwork, and coffee tables.

The golden section is a series of ratios that are often employed to help determine proper window proportions and room sizes, but they can also be used in selecting the right-sized accessories and artwork. Commonly used golden ratios include 2:3, 3:5, 4:7, and 5:8. These ratios set up a balance of symmetry and asymmetry between spaces and shapes. To illustrate this in action, picture a wall that is eight feet wide. Using the 5:8 ratio, a five-foot wide entertainment center or dresser would be a good fit. If a large piece in the right size is not available, try combining several furniture pieces, plants, or accessories.

The golden mean establishes that dividing an area's length somewhere between one-half and one-third is the most pleasing visually. This is especially helpful when dealing with accessory placement and tying back window treatments. Instead of choosing the middle of a drapery as the tie-back point, it is more appealing to go just above or below the midpoint.

The ancient Greeks also found that groupings of odd numbers were more satisfying than even numbers of objects. For example, one or three throw pillows on a sofa will be more interesting than two.

Later in this chapter you will find a variety of resources and ideas which can help you quickly develop the design knowledge that can help you succeed in the home staging business.

3.1.2 Business Skills

If you are well prepared for being a business owner, your home staging business is more likely to be a success.

> *"People often enter the industry and treat it as a hobby, which is great for those wanting a supplemental income. For those looking to build a business that will support you, your family, and provide an adequate retirement, you'd better be willing and able to run a business.*
>
> *Staging is much more than just removing clutter and neutralizing walls. Running a successful staging business takes all the skills of running any business. You have to be a sales person, marketer, web designer, furniture mover, bookkeeper… or at least have the ability to bring those people in to*

help you. One thing is certain, unlike the years I spent working in corporate America, I still wake up every morning and love going to work!"

— Jason Maxwell, president,
Dallas chapter of the International Association of Home Staging Professionals

Running a successful home staging business requires a variety of business skills. You will need to know about:

- Business planning
- Financial management
- Operations management
- Inventory management
- Hiring and supervising employees
- Marketing and sales

While you don't have to learn it all, it's crucial to know where your business stands financially at all times. Staying on top of your accounting will help you avoid finding yourself in the awful position of being out of cash to pay your bills. The more you can keep your expenses down while building a solid customer base to build revenues, the more successful your home staging business will be.

For some of these tasks, you can hire employees or contractors to help you, such as a bookkeeper or someone who can handle the marketing and promotion for your business. Keep in mind, though, that the fewer people you need to hire to help you manage your business, the lower your overall costs of running the business. Developing business skills takes time, so don't be in such a rush that you neglect to fill in any gaps in your knowledge or skills.

Any business related experience you have can be helpful, and there are a number of ways you can develop your skills and knowledge in all of these areas. In this chapter, you'll find specific ideas to help you increase your experience and knowledge of running a home staging business. You'll also find detailed advice throughout the remaining sections of this guide.

You will probably find reading the entire guide before you launch your business helpful, but you can quickly identify particular areas you may want to focus on by reviewing the table of contents. For example, section 4.2 gives you advice about financial management of a home staging business, from start-up financing to setting your fees.

One tool for helping you to focus on what business skills are involved in being a business owner is business planning. Section 4.1.1 looks in detail at how to develop a business plan to get your business up and running by outlining and clarifying what services you will offer, deciding how you will finance your business, creating a market plan, etc. In addition to addressing these important business issues, a business plan will also help you to understand some of the other basic "hard" skills required of a business owner, such as marketing and accounting skills.

Resources for Developing Business Skills

The following resources can help you develop your business skills:

SBA

The Small Business Administration (SBA) is a leading U.S. government resource for information about licensing, taxes, and starting a small business. You can find a range of resources including information on financing your new business, business plans and much more at **www.sba.gov**.

SCORE

The Service Corps of Retired Executives (SCORE) is an organization of U.S. volunteers who donate their time and expertise to new business owners. You can find information on taxes, tips for starting your business, or even find a mentor who will coach you and help you maximize your chances of succeeding as a new business owner. Visit them at **www.score.org**.

Canada Business Service Centers

This Canadian government website offers information on legislation, taxes, incorporation, and other issues of interest to Canadian business owners or those who do business in Canada. For more information and a list of services they offer visit their website at **www.canadabusiness.ca**.

3.1.3 Interpersonal Skills

As a home stager, you will need effective interpersonal skills to help you develop relationships with a wide variety of people. That's because you won't be working in an office with the same staff from week to week as in a traditional 9-to-5 job. This daily variety can have its ups and downs. The good news is you'll be meeting diverse, interesting people on a regular basis. The bad news is you'll need to charm a wide range of personalities, from easy-going to anxious and everything in between.

Relationship Building

As you work with homeowners, you will develop friendships and close relationships along the way. Understandably, emotions can run high when a client is preparing to transfer ownership of their home, probably one of their largest financial investments. You should project a professional, relaxed demeanor with your clients, and be sure to cultivate your skills in dealing with sticky situations.

Take the time to build a rapport with your clients by briefly engaging in small talk about their neighborhood or family interests. This information will not only build a social connection, it will also provide insight into your client's personal preferences and style.

Since you will be working in the private homes of your clients, it's imperative that you maintain a high level of discretion. Gossiping or complaining about a client's personality, family life, or home condition is by no means a good idea. You never know who could be an acquaintance of your client—it's a small world after all!

When dealing with subcontractors in the presence of your client, it's best not to have uncomfortable disagreements. If there is a problem with a subcontractor's service or behavior, take them aside privately or have the discussion with them later at another location. Your clients and subcontractors will appreciate the professional way you deal with issues when they arise.

If you would like to improve your relationship building skills, an excellent resource is the classic book *How to Win Friends and Influence People,* by Dale Carnegie.

Communication Skills

Communication skills are key to building effective interpersonal relationships. Face-to-face interpersonal communication can be classified as one-to-one, small group, or public. Generally speaking, you will most frequently encounter one-to-one communication at client consultations or when working with subcontractors.

Occasionally, you'll meet a client along with their spouse or other family members. When communicating with small groups of three or more people, pay close attention to the roles that emerge during the conversation. Who is the decision maker? What is important to each person?

Public communication includes presenting or speaking to a large, assembled group such as giving a speech at a local Chamber of Commerce meeting to educate the audience about your staging services. You can learn how to use public speaking to market your services as a home stager in section 5.3.4 in this guide.

Effectively communication is a two-way process of speaking and listening. In a typical client conversation, you will ask your clients what they want, listen closely to your client's stated needs, and then acknowledge that you understand what has been conveyed. As Joanne Hans of A Perfect Placement says: "You always have to keep the lines of communication open. Make sure you and the client are on the same page." Here are some tips on improving interpersonal communication skills:

Listening

Being an excellent listener is key to providing your clients with the service they want. While listening seems like an easy skill to master, most of us experience challenges in at least one of the following areas involved in listening: paying attention, understanding, and remembering.

If you need more information on what a client needs or wants, ask open-ended questions rather than yes or no questions. For example, asking

"What colors would you like to see in this room?" leads to more information than simply asking "Do you like yellow?"

You can become a better listener by focusing fully on someone when they are speaking. Here are some ways to do that:

- Don't interrupt the other person. Hear them out.
- Keep listening to the other person, even if you think you know what they will say next. If you make assumptions, you may miss the point they're making.
- Ask questions in order to clarify what the other person has said. Take notes if necessary.
- Don't be distracted by outside interference. Loud noises, the other person mispronouncing a word, or even an uncomfortable room temperature can break your concentration and distract you from the conversation.
- Give feedback to the other person. Nod occasionally; say things like "I see," and smile, if appropriate. Let them know you're listening.
- Use paraphrasing. In other words, repeat back in your own words your understanding of what the other person has said. It can help alleviate misunderstandings later on.

If this is a skill you want to improve, there are numerous books on the subject of honing your listening skills and one of the best is *Listening: The Forgotten Skill (A Self-Teaching Guide)*, by Madelyn Burley-Allen. Helpful free advice is available online at **www.businesslistening.com**.

Verbal Communication Skills

Good verbal skills are helpful when you are selling yourself to potential clients or when you need to communicate with employees, suppliers, or other business people, such as your banker. Many people prefer to work with somebody they can understand who "speaks their language."

As someone who will be paid to point out and minimize a home's flaws, you'll need to develop a talent for thoughtfully communicating why something won't work and what will work better. You should be confident and decisive when sharing your suggestions, but also be willing to compromise or yield if your client doesn't like a particular idea.

In addition, when evaluating a client's belongings, be careful not to denigrate any items that may seem useless or outdated, as they might have sentimental value. Start by asking, "Is this item special to you?" If they express that the item is just junk or clutter, then you can speak more freely about it. If the item does have a special place in their life, recommend a solution for storing or displaying the item, so that it will fit within the room's look.

> **TIP:** To improve your verbal communication skills, ask friends or a vocal coach for feedback on any areas that could be improved, such as: clarity of speech, use of slang, proper grammar, or altering your tone of voice to eliminate any harshness. (You can find vocal coaches in the Yellow Pages.)

Reading Non-Verbal Messages

Nonverbal communication (tone of voice, facial expression, body language, etc.) will also play an important role during your client meetings. Maintain a comfortable level of eye contact with your clients during conversations and use active posture when listening to them. Nodding along as your clients describe their situation will express that you hear and understand them. Take note of their facial expressions, gestures, and voice intonation as you gauge their reactions to your ideas. These signals can give you valuable clues about what the other person is thinking.

Being able to "read" people can not only help you get the job, but can also help ensure you keep your clients satisfied. For example, did a prospective client fold their arms when you made a particular suggestion? If so, they may be communicating that they disagree, even if they don't actually say so.

Although body language can't tell you precisely what someone is thinking, it can give you clues so you can ask follow-up questions, even as basic as "How do you feel about that?" If you want to improve this skill, you can find some excellent advice in books such as *Reading People,* by Jo-Ellan Dimitrius, Ph.D. and Mark Mazzarella, and *How to Read a Person Like a Book,* by Gerald I. Nierenberg and Henry H. Calero.

3.1.4 Other Useful Skills to Have

Working as a home stager will call for a knowledge of home decorating techniques, business skills, and a variety of interpersonal skills as we've learned. In addition, you will need some of the following "soft" skills.

Problem Solving Ability

As you will quickly discover, creative thinking and problem-solving go hand-in-hand, so being able to come up with a solution or remedy to reach a goal is perhaps one of the most fundamental traits that a home stager can develop.

In this field, you will be a problem solver on many levels. Homeowners will come to you with their initial problem: selling their home quickly for the most profit possible. You will evaluate their property before staging begins, and find ways to quickly and economically fix any problem areas.

Every room in a staged house will almost certainly require problem solving on some level. For example, you may ponder how to make a client's bedroom look larger. Remove the frame on their four-poster bed, get rid of the clutter, and the problem's solved! You can develop your home staging problem-solving skills through experience. Section 3.2 offers ideas for a variety of ways you can start to get hands-on experience.

Patience and Flexibility

As a business owner, there will be moments when it all may seem like too much to handle. A real estate agent or homeowner may have unrealistic expectations, or there may be another contractor holding up your progress on a project.

If you find yourself in need of more patience, try practicing a technique that works for you. Counting to ten before reacting to a frustrating situation may help soothe the anxiety. Patience will also come in handy when a last-minute change of plans is needed or a new issue is tossed into the mix.

This flexibility, or being responsive to change, will make your projects go more smoothly. When you are in the middle of a major project it can be hard to "switch horses in midstream," as the saying goes. Allowing those gears to shift in your mind and adapting to new developments will be key.

Organizational Ability

Keeping all the daily details of your business in order will increase your efficiency and also give you peace of mind. You will likely have four or five clients at the same time (maybe even more), whose houses are in different phases of home staging. You must have a system for tracking the progress of all your projects and for keeping in touch with your clients. Organizing client files and paperwork will be easier if you start with standard file folders and keep an alphabetized system. Make a folder for each new client and then arrange the files from A to Z in a filing cabinet or file box.

Purchase a personal calendar or day planner to manage your appointments, to-do lists, contacts, and client notes. I like planners that show each week's schedule in a two-page spread, so that I can get a quick feel for the week ahead. There are also day planners that break down each day into hourly increments for more in-depth scheduling.

You may find it useful to have two calendars and two client lists. This duplicate system protects you in case your working calendar or client list is ever misplaced. An efficient way to accomplish this would be to create a calendar and client list on your personal computer and then print out your data as needed. Also, it's always a good idea to create back-up copies of important computer files on a flash drive or CD.

Organizational ability will also be useful during the initial stages of your home staging projects. As we've outlined in section 2.5, organizing your clients' possessions is an important component of depersonalizing their homes. Keeping them organized by introducing an organizational system into their lives will help to maintain your design's neutrality during the period their homes are for sale.

To learn professional organizing techniques, you can take a course. A few of these are listed in section 3.4. Of course, you don't need to become a professional organizer in order to be successful as a home stager. However, a basic knowledge of some of the techniques used by professional organizers will help you to more quickly assess and dispose of clients' organizational issues. You can also find a few organizing websites in section 3.5, if you would like to read more about this field on your own.

3.2 Learning by Doing

Building your knowledge of home staging will be the main focus of your activities in the early stages of launching your business. Practicing your skills will give you a chance to build a design portfolio which will be important to winning over new clients. Moreover, the time you spend exploring different segments of the industry will allow you to define your preferred target market and niche services.

3.2.1 Find Home Decorating or Design Work

A practical way to become more proficient at home staging is to spend some time working in the design industry. You will become familiar with ordering products from manufacturers, and discover which neighborhoods generate the best clients. You'll also get paid in the process. Look for opportunities in all segments of the business, such as:

Design Studios and Firms

You should be able to find local interior designers with a studio or showroom that focuses on residential or commercial design. Either way, this is a perfect place to become an intern or assistant. Keep in mind however that these are coveted jobs, so there may be a lot of competition for just a few positions.

Architectural Firms

Along with designing homes and commercial structures, most architects also have staff interior designers who finish out their new buildings or remodeling projects. These designers may be seeking entry-level candidates to help coordinate any projects that are in progress.

Manufacturers

You may want to consider being a sales representative with a window covering, furniture, flooring, or fabric maker. There may be a few manufacturers in your area, or you can call the corporate headquarters of any manufacturer and ask if they are looking for reps in your region. In this type of position, you will gain product knowledge direct from the source and will be on a first-name basis with most of the designers in your area. Manufacturer reps often end up working for the businesses that were previously on their sales route.

Real Estate Agents

Working as an assistant at a realtor's office would be a good fit for any aspiring home stager, since many agents now offer staging services along with listing a property for sale. If they like your work, they will think about using you for all their listings. For properties that have recently sold, the real estate agent can also recommend your redesign services to help the buyers set up their new house.

3.2.2 Find Decorating-Related Work

Furniture Stores

Many home furnishings companies, including international retailer Bassett Furniture Direct, now offer free decorating services to their patrons. This complimentary design help is carried out in-store or even in the customer's home. As more furniture stores jump on this bandwagon, there will be a demand for employees with an interest or prior training in decorating concepts. (To see Bassett's career page, go to **www.bassett furniture.com/company/careers/index.asp**.)

Floral Designers

Florists often lend a hand to interior designers and decorators by crafting silk and live arrangements for private homes as well as commercial spaces like restaurants and hotels. While working with a floral designer, you will learn how to make your own floral displays and get a chance to practice color coordination. When staging a house, especially a vacant house, floral arrangements will be an important element for creating an inviting and interesting space.

Art and Accessory Boutiques

Smaller retailers carrying artwork or hip home accessories have a challenge when merchandising their stores because of limited space. Boutique owners have a need for creative people who like accessorizing on an everyday basis to keep their shops fresh and interesting.

Home Décor Retailers

Companies like Pier 1 Imports and The Bombay Company sell products with a distinctive style that their customers find irresistible. Bigger than a boutique, yet not quite a department store, these home fashion chains want employees who can attractively group furniture and accessories for mass appeal. You can visit Pier 1's career page at **www.pier1.com/SideMenu/Careers/tabid/69/Default.aspx**. The Bombay Company closed its stores in the U.S. in early 2008, but still operates in Canada. Visit their career page at **www.bombay.ca/pages.php?pageid=19**.

You can find a listing of other similar retailers, as well as department stores, in section 2.2. Look for their "Careers" page link (usually located at the bottom of the home page), or use the "Contact Us" link.

Department Stores

These large multi-department retailers present an opportunity to handle products made for almost every room in a house. Assisting a store merchandiser or window display designer would be terrific experience for a home stager, but much of this work is usually done after store hours when new inventory is set out.

Some department stores even have specific positions for designers or decorators. For example, JCPenney stores have window treatment and home fashion departments with on-staff decorating consultants who work in the stores and also make client house calls. JCPenney provides initial training and even conducts continual training as needed. To see available career opportunities at JCPenney, go to **www.jcpenney.net/careers/N3_stores/default.aspx** and click on "Custom Decorating."

Special Event Planners

These multitaskers work with professionals from a wide range of fields including floral designers and interior decorators. Special event planners coordinate all the aspects of an occasion, including visual elements like décor, color schemes, tablescape design, and lighting design.

They often work with floral designers in planning and arranging tablescapes, which is a great exercise in the art of vignette staging. Also, the venues for special events range from homes to hotel ballrooms and everything in between, so you will have the opportunity to sharpen your knack for space planning.

Home Improvement Retailers

At mega-stores like Lowe's and Home Depot, employees rotate through a variety of home décor departments like window blinds, paint, flooring, kitchens, baths, wallpaper, and lighting. This diverse training is a speedy way to find out about all the top products and techniques for your client's projects.

Home Party Shows

Becoming a direct sales consultant for a company like Signature HomeStyles (**www.signaturehomestyles.com**) or Celebrating Home (**www.celebratinghome.com**) involves selling home décor products through a party format in people's homes. You can earn money while demonstrating your decorating talents to a room full of potential staging clients.

3.2.3 Volunteer Your Services

There are many other ways to get experience in decorating and design work. One of the best ways to get some practical experience in a low-pressure setting is by doing a project for family or friends. Here are some ideas for volunteering your services:

Volunteer Your Services to Friends and Family

One of the most supportive environments to try out your new skills can be in the homes of people who know you best. Your friends and family members will encourage your efforts and will probably be thrilled to have some free decorating advice.

Be sure to take "before and after" photos of all the projects completed in the homes of friends and family, so that you can build up your design portfolio.

Stage a Friend's or Relative's House for Free

Almost all of us know someone who is selling a home or thinking about it in the near future and, if they are open to the idea, you can offer your services to them for free. Start with a consultation just like you would with a paying client, then go through each step in the staging process. Not only will this be good practice, but your friend or relative will supply priceless word-of-mouth advertising at every social function after the house sells quickly and for more money than they expected.

Offer Redesign Services to Friends or Relatives

This flexible decorating service can be applied to one problem room or to their whole house. Exhibiting your creativity with what they already own will get your friends and family talking about your services. You can even include color suggestions and ideas for new items if they are interested.

Remodeling Projects

There is a good possibility that someone you are acquainted with is in the middle of planning or completing a remodeling project. These in-depth projects can take weeks or months to fully finish and involve a lot of variables, so your assistance likely will be welcomed.

Party Décor and Table Settings

Friendly gatherings and family functions are the perfect showcase for revealing your decorative flair. Planning party décor and table settings that are memorable and unique will make your creations a hot topic of discussion. Start with a theme, develop a color palette, and include plenty of small details like coordinated invitations or custom place card holders. By orchestrating an event's food, flowers, and decorative details, you will rehearse home staging techniques such as building appealing vignettes.

Holiday Decorating

Sprucing up your friend's and relative's homes with holiday decorations is another enjoyable way to display your abilities. Whether it's for Christmas, Halloween, Easter, or Thanksgiving, the whole house from curb to backyard can be festooned for the season. In fact, there are even decorators who specialize in this specific area of seasonal decorating.

Shopping Excursions

Joining your family members or friends on shopping trips for furniture and accessories is a wonderful opportunity to help them save time and money by volunteering your expertise. Your trained eye will recognize diamonds in the rough at flea markets, antique stores, retail shops, and fabric stores.

These outings are also a chance to see what shopping trips with clients will be like, since this is another service you can provide along with home staging. An alternative to shopping with clients is to act as their personal shopper. Busy clients will appreciate the option of having someone to go shopping on their behalf.

3.2.4 Evaluate Home Design Locally

A different avenue for learning this job is to actively evaluate homes and public spaces in your area. Browse and study the vignettes of local design studios, upscale furniture stores, and home accessory boutiques. In the quest to entice shoppers to open up their wallets, retailers spend a lot of time and money merchandising their wares. While window shopping or strolling through a store, you will likely see some unique ideas for positioning furniture and arranging accessories.

Model houses constructed in new neighborhoods are another excellent resource because their décor is carefully planned for a broad audience of home buyers. The techniques used in these interiors will be directly applicable to staging your clients' homes for sale.

You should also seek out a "tour of homes" or "parade of homes" event in your area. These tours are usually held once or twice a year, and they highlight a collection of beautifully decorated homes in a coordinated tour format. Show homes or dream houses are a related type of model home that is hosted by a builder or civic group, often to benefit a charitable cause. In addition, you may find breathtaking historical homes that are open to public tours.

3.3 Learning From Other Home Staging Professionals

3.3.1 Information Interviews

Experts from just about any industry who have become successful business owners or leaders can become dependable sources for advice and inspiration. Seeking out these professionals is worthwhile and will be instrumental to your success in starting and growing a business. While you may initially search for experts in the interior design or real estate industries, don't be afraid to look for successful people from a diverse mix of backgrounds.

When contemplating the move to the home staging industry, it's smart to have discussions with the people actually working in that field. Informational interviews are brief meetings with individuals who have experience in the line of work that you are pursuing. Your role in these meetings will be to set them up and to start off the conversation with sensibly-chosen questions. Such interviews will present you with a realistic view of this career, help you refine your service offerings, and allow you to assemble a network of industry contacts.

But where do you begin? While the potential candidates for informational interviews are almost limitless, you can start with these groups and see where it leads you:

- Family members, friends, neighbors, and acquaintances
- Teachers, professors, and guidance counselors (previous or current)
- Classmates or coworkers (previous or current)
- People mentioned in newspaper articles or on TV broadcasts
- Members of professional organizations related to this field
- Business owners who focus on similar or related services (check the Yellow Pages or local business directories)

When you've decided on a person to contact for an interview, you'll have the option to simply pick up the phone, or you can write an introductory letter or email. If you are contacting someone who spends time at a retail or office location, you could even stop by in person to ask for an informational interview. In your request for a meeting be sure to:

- Briefly introduce yourself
- Mention how you found or were referred to this person
- Explain that you are seeking career advice and industry information (be specific)
- Ask for only twenty to thirty minutes of their time

After you land an interview with one of your contacts, you should prepare a list of questions to take along with you. Remember to dress professionally and be considerate of the person's time. After all, you may hear of an internship or job prospect during your informational interview. Nevertheless, your most important goal will be gathering insider industry information.

You may want to include some of the following questions in your interview:

- What is your average day like?
- How did you break into home staging?
- What do you like the most about home staging?
- What do you dislike about home staging?
- What are the average incomes for people starting out?
- What personality traits do you feel are important as a home stager?
- What type of skills should I develop?
- What does the future look like for the home staging industry?
- Do you have any advice for newcomers?

During this brief informational dialogue, your interviewee may suggest other people to contact for further discussions. If they don't offer first, feel free to inquire about other interview subjects, so that you can keep growing your contact list. Be sure to send a thank-you note after your meeting to thank your new contact for their time and candor in talking about their industry.

3.3.2 Mentoring

While informational interviews are exceptional resources, you will hit the career jackpot by landing a mentor who will work with you on a continuing basis. A mentor is someone whose knowledge and success qualifies them to counsel or teach an aspiring protégé.

You might find that one of your informational interviewees is open to being your industry mentor or business coach. A healthy mentoring partnership will allow both you and your mentor to find new inspiration and experience individual growth.

Here are a few tips for finding your perfect mentorship:

- Be your own public relations firm by mentioning your business plans to your friends, family, coworkers, and colleagues. Try asking them for a mentor recommendation. Be sure they understand your goals and what type of person you're seeking.

- Casual acquaintances encountered everyday in your community may hold an untapped supply of expert advice. Strike up a conversation with the manager at the local dry cleaners or have a chat with the regulars at your gym. You could find that some of these people are willing to share their knowledge in accounting, legal matters, or other business-related issues with which they are familiar.

- Since the basic principles of business ownership are universal, you should connect with successful entrepreneurs in whatever field you find them. They will be able to share what worked and didn't work in building their business, so that you can apply their lessons to your own industry.

- Look to your past mentors or those who had a profound influence on your life. Figure out why this person was a good fit with your personality and keep these qualities in mind for sizing up a career mentor.

- There's no rule that says you can only have one mentor at a time. Learn from an eclectic mix of people who each focus on different areas of your development. You may end up with a business coach, a friend who helps hone your people skills, and a fellow home stager who gives you project-specific advice.
- After pinpointing a mentorship contender, you can convince them to take you under their wing by asking insightful questions and actively listening. By displaying a sincere interest in your potential mentor and their expertise, they will probably want to help you succeed.

If your local mentorship bank is running low on funds, there are some other alternatives to find a nurturing match. Organizations like the Small Business Development Center and SCORE are good places to start. The programs of the Small Business Development Center (SBDC) provide free counseling and business guidance to entrepreneurs at over 1,100 local centers across the United States. Each local SBDC office recruits a broad range of mentors to volunteer their expertise. To find more information, visit **www.asbdc-us.org**.

SCORE (**www.score.org**) the self-proclaimed "Counselors to America's Small Business," offers free and impartial counseling to entrepreneurs nationwide. SCORE has over 11,000 volunteers who are accessible online and 400 local chapter offices where you can meet in person with a counselor. Go to **www.score.org/findscore** to locate a local SCORE chapter office near you.

3.3.3 Join Associations

You may bump into a potential mentor at a local meeting of a professional association. Better yet, you could land a new client or find a business opportunity through your networking with the association's members.

A professional association is an organized group of people with the shared purpose of advancing a certain industry or occupation. Most associations operate as non-profits and endeavor to educate their members while upholding a set of ethics among their peers. Some associations are also active lobbyists who support the collective political interests of their members.

When launching your business, you should give some thought to joining a professional association specializing in small business or entrepreneurship. At the least, you should study the wealth of information on their websites and perhaps go to a local meeting, if there is one being held in your area.

There are also numerous professional associations that are specific to the interior design industry and its related fields. A number of these groups provide industry certification or exclusive training to their members. Keep in mind, most of the home staging associations will require you to complete one of their training programs in order to become a registered member. Being a member of a design related association will give you a built-in network of mentors and advisors who have direct experience with your line of business.

You should study what each group has to offer and weigh the potential benefits of membership against the costs. For example, having a relationship with a well-respected association may boost your appeal with clients, but it may involve a large investment in money or time. Even after your initial enrollment, there may be quarterly or annual dues to consider.

On the other hand, becoming a member of a prosperous, established design community might be just the spark needed to ignite your business. This outcome will be more likely if the association continually drives clients to you through their own marketing and referral efforts. Make the association work for you!

Home Staging Associations

- *International Association of Home Staging Professionals (IAHSP)*
  www.iahsp.com

- *Real Estate Staging Association*
  www.realestatestagingassociation.com

- *Canadian Redesigners Association (CRDA)*
  www.canadianredesigners.org

Interior Design and Decorating Associations

- *American Society of Interior Designers (ASID)*
  The oldest and largest professional association for residential and commercial interior designers
  www.asid.org

- *International Interior Design Association (IIDA)*
  www.iida.org

- *Interior Design Society (IDS)*
  The largest professional association devoted solely to residential interior design.
  www.interiordesignsociety.org

- *Interior Designers of Canada (IDC)*
  www.interiordesigncanada.org

- *Certified Interior Decorators International (CID)*
  www.cidinternational.org

Interior Decorators vs. Interior Designers

The use of the term "interior designer" is generally reserved for those individuals with a college level education or equivalent in the subject, and they must comply with nationwide state licensing requirements. Interior designers offer additional services and expertise related to architectural or structural elements in a house or building.

If you will be seeking a college level degree in interior design, make sure the program is accredited by the Council for Interior Design Accreditation (**www.accredit-id.org**), formerly known as FIDER. For over 35 years, they have held rank as an independent accrediting group for interior design education at colleges and universities in both the U.S. and Canada.

American Society of Interior Designers (ASID) membership is open to those who have completed a two or four year college degree in interior design. Their highest level of membership also mandates that applicants pass the NCIDQ exam (**www.ncidq.org**). States and provinces with licensing requirements have chosen this rigorous test as the standard qualification for aspiring interior designers.

What It Means to be "Certified"

Since there are no industry governing groups for home staging, the value of any certifications in these fields is dependent on the strength of the group hosting the program. Although the terms "certified" and "accredited" are used in many of the available training workshops, there are no standard qualifications to work in home staging. No impartial third party organization like NCIDQ is monitoring and evaluating those who have taken these training programs, so they are not required in order for you to call yourself a home stager. However, being certified by a training program does show your clients that you have invested time and effort in learning your trade.

Certification will not guarantee results unless your portfolio and personal selling skills are up to par. Debra Gould, president of Six Elements, believes that "the issue is not your credentials, since none exist, but whether you know how to build your credibility and market your services effectively."

To help fill the void of independent certification for interior decorators, Certified Interior Decorators International (**www.cidinternational.org**) launched itself in 1997. In order to use the trademarked title of Certified Interior Decorator, applicants must complete an approved study course and pass an entrance exam.

Other professional associations that are worth checking out include:

- *National Association of Professional Organizers (NAPO)*
  www.napo.net

- *Professional Organizers in Canada (POC)*
  www.organizersincanada.com

- *National Association for the Self-Employed*
  www.nase.org

- *Association for Enterprise Opportunity*
  www.microenterpriseworks.org

- *American Marketing Association – Small Business Strategy*
  www.marketingpower.com

- *National Association of Women Business Owners*
  www.nawbo.org

- *Women Entrepreneurs of Canada*
  www.wec.ca

Another type of professional association that can be found in almost every community is the local Chamber of Commerce. These business-oriented groups present opportunities for networking, visibility, and skill growth through their seminars and programs. Additionally, chamber members often pursue economic development projects that lure new businesses into their communities and encourage a vibrant local economy.

Find your local Chamber of Commerce by searching at the U.S. Chamber of Commerce Directory (**www.uschamber.com/chambers/directory**) or the International Chamber of Commerce Directory (**www.chamberfind.com**).

3.4 Training Programs and Workshops

In order to heighten your confidence and professional know-how, you should think about enrolling in a program or seminar that specializes in the art of home staging, redesign, or interior decorating. While some programs are more expensive than others, a lofty price tag does not automatically guarantee a high quality program.

Since each course has something different to offer, you should vigilantly research the cost versus the actual curriculum before making a decision. When you locate a training workshop that is a good fit for your personality and career goals, there are numerous benefits to be gleaned from the experience.

This section will explain the existing opportunities for education and give you an idea of what to expect from each program.

3.4.1 What a Program or Workshop Should Offer

If you spend some time searching for training in this industry, you will quickly discover an overwhelming assortment of available options. Because there is no official governing body over home staging, just about anybody can market courses and their own certifications in these specialties. All the more reason to do your homework.

A good training program should give you practical advice to use in the field and connect you with a group of like-minded peers who can form a support group or even lead to potential business partners. When evaluating each workshop, take into account the following criteria:

Classroom Lecture

Whether the format is in a classroom, over the Internet, or over the phone, this core part of any instructional program will deliver direct advice from your instructor and usually a printed course outline that you can reference later.

Hands-on Training

Many of the home staging training sessions include actual projects inside practice homes. For those who are still timid about performing these services, this may be a golden opportunity. If you are someone who is already comfortable working in a client's home, this step may not be necessary.

Business Start-up and Marketing Guidance

As you can see from their prominent inclusion in this guide, understanding these topics is crucial in this line of work. Many training programs may gloss over issues like starting up and marketing your business. On the other hand, whatever advice is presented should be tailored to your specific field, so it could be very useful. For the most part, growing a business in any service industry is strongly rooted in positive word-of-mouth advertising from satisfied customers.

On-going Support

Any program worth its salt will grant you on-going support for any questions or issues that may arise in the course of building your business. This support might range from direct access to your instructor to online forums where graduates of the program help each other. The most valuable option is to be assigned a successful mentor who can be easily reached as needed.

Advertising

Another area of on-going support is the marketing that an organization does to promote the industry or more importantly their program. If they do a good job referring clients to their list of graduates, this will be a lucrative benefit. Inquire about the marketing and advertising activities they pursue and find out what kind of traffic their website receives in an average month.

Certificates or Diplomas

Having a piece of paper that describes the training you have undergone is a great addition to your portfolio. You can also mention this training on your marketing materials such as business cards, brochures, and website. The perceived value of this training is up to each client to decide, but choosing a program that is a nice fit for you and your target market will help.

Graduates and Former Students

If you are considering enrollment in a training program, the most important thing you can do is to contact graduates of the course. Many of the training websites also feature directory listings of their members. Look up a few former students of the program, and then call or email them to ask their opinion on the training they received.

3.4.2 Home Staging Workshops and Seminars

While there may be new options sprouting up everyday, there are a collection of training programs that have helped to establish the staging field. It is essential that you evaluate any course before enrolling, so that you know how it stacks up against the other seminars out there.

In general, the available workshops last anywhere from two to five days and feature a combination of classroom instruction and hands-on projects. To give you a head start on your research, here are a few of the leading courses being marketed today:

Staged Homes

Accredited Staging Professional Course (ASP)

Website:	**www.stagedhomes.com**
Location:	Offers 3-day training workshops across North America. Check the ASP course schedule on the website to find a workshop near you.
Cost:	$1,795
Contact:	Email **ASPCourses@StagedHomes.com** or phone 1-800-392-7161

Use What You Have

Interior Refiner and Resale-Ready Programs

Website:	**www.redecorate.com/training.html**
Location:	New York City
Cost:	$3,500 for 5-day session (not including airfare or hotel)
Contact:	Email **info@redecorate.com** or phone 1-800-938-7348

Realty Enhancement International

Realty Enhancement Specialist Course (RES)

Website:	**www.realtyenhancements.com/training.html**
Location:	Irvine, California
Cost:	$2,200 for a 3-day seminar
Contact:	Email **wdilda@AOL.com**

Certified Staging Professional (CSP)

Website: **www.csptraining.com**

Location: Across the U.S. and Canada; also offered in Australia

Cost: $1,999 for a 3-day (30 hours) seminar

Contact: Email **lori@stagingtraining.com** or **liz@stagingtraining.com**

Canadian Redesigners Association (CRDA)

Website: **www.canadianredesigners.org**

Location: Offered in British Columbia, Saskatchewan, and Ontario.

Cost: $2,000 (plus GST) for a 5-day course

Contact: Visit **www.canadianredesigners.org/index.cfm?DocID=14501** to find contact information for a course in your area.

Canadian Staging Professionals

Website: **www.canadianstagingprofessionals.com/t_training_stager.php**

Location: Alberta, B.C, New Brunswick, Nova Scotia and Ontario

Cost: $1,999 for a 3-day (30 hours) course

Contact: **linda@stagingtraining.ca**

3.4.3 Online and Correspondence Courses

Are you on a tight budget, or is your schedule too hectic to get away for a multi-day seminar? Maybe your current skill level means that you can do without the classroom experience or the hands-on practice.

In any case, a training program with an online or correspondence format may be right up your alley. If you decide that one of these more flexible workshops is right for you, begin your research with programs like the following:

Use What You Have

At Home Decorator Training Program

Website:	**www.redecorate.com**
Format:	Can be taken online or as a five-day session (limited enrollment in New York City)
Cost:	$2,000 for the online course or $3,500 for the NYC session
Contact:	Email **info@redecorate.com** or phone 1-800-938-7348

The Staging Diva®

Home Staging Business Training Program

Website:	**www.stagingdiva.com**
Format:	Audio recordings on CD of five courses, with accompanying workbooks, or you can download all the materials online.
Cost:	$249 per course or all five for $995 available for download, or a home study course including all five courses for $1,295 (you can pay for the home study kit in three installments).
Contact:	Email **debra@stagingdiva.com** or phone 1-416-691-6615

Home Staging Expert, HSE

Home Study Course Option

Website:	**www.homestagingexpert.com/training.htm**
Format:	Online or as 2-day or 4-day (Minneapolis only) workshops
Cost:	$299 for the online course, $750 for the 2-day workshop, and $1,499 for the 4-day Minneapolis workshop
Contact:	Email **info@homestagingexpert.com** or phone 1-651-220-2746

For those interested in a two or four year degree in interior design that can be completed over the Internet, colleges like the Art Institute (**www.aionline.edu**) now have coursework for just such a purpose.

3.4.4 Other Staging Related Courses

Business Courses

Earning a degree, diploma, or certificate in business can be helpful in running your own business, but you don't need to go quite as far as getting a Bachelor of Commerce degree or an MBA. A formal business education is not necessary to run a successful home staging business.

There are many successful business owners who are self-taught and have never studied business. However, the skills you learn in business classes can come in handy. Depending on which of your skills you would like to develop, consider taking courses on topics such as:

- Advertising
- Basic Accounting
- Business Communications
- Business Management
- Entrepreneurship
- Merchandising
- Retailing

Your local college or university may offer these and other business courses. Through the continuing education department you may be able to take a single course on a Saturday or over several evenings. If you can't find a listing for the continuing education department in your local phone book, call the college's main switchboard and ask for the continuing education department. They will be able to tell you about upcoming courses. If you would like to learn more about business concepts, you can find information and links to colleges and universities at Peterson's Planner at **www.petersons.com**, or in Canada, you can visit the Schoolfinder website at **www.schoolfinder.com**.

If you are not interested in attending courses at a school, or you don't have the time, another option that can easily fit into your schedule is distance learning. Traditionally these were called correspondence courses and the lessons were mailed back and forth between student and instructor. Today, with the help of the Internet, there are many online courses available. Again, check your local community college, university, or business school to see if they offer online courses.

Your local Chamber of Commerce may also offer training courses and seminars for new business owners. Many also offer consultations with retired executives and business owners who are well-qualified to offer advice. Visit **www.chamberofcommerce.com** to find a chamber near you.

Home Organizing Courses

A good place to start looking for classes and seminars in home organizing is at the websites of the professional associations and other websites dedicated to professional organizing. Many of the members of these associations offer such classes. Here is a list of places to start looking for professional organizers in your area:

- *National Association of Professional Organizers Member Directory*
  www.napo.net/referral/

- *Professional Organizers in Canada Classes and Other Events*
  www.organizersincanada.com/poc_events.php

- *Professional Organizers Webring*
  www.organizerswebring.com/members/default.asp

3.5 Resources for Self-Study

Probably the most affordable and flexible way to gain knowledge of interior decorating concepts is to study independently via TV shows, books, magazines, and websites. You should sample all these media to achieve a well-rounded perspective. This is a customizable learning approach because you choose when, where, and what information you will examine. It can also be a time-saver because you can survey just the programs or titles that are relevant to the services you intend to offer.

3.5.1 Staging and Design TV Shows

Staging and design shows provide a pressure-free way to pick up unique decorating ideas and helpful tips for working with clients. These programs typically feature real clients and experienced designers who take you through the decorating process step-by-step. While there are countless design shows currently on the air, the programs listed below feature staging and redesign concepts:

- *Clean Sweep – Home Organization Makeover Show*
  http://tlc.discovery.com/fansites/cleansweep/cleansweep.html

- *Designed to Sell – Home Staging Makeover Show*
  www.hgtv.com/designed-to-sell/show/

- *Get It Sold*
  www.hgtv.com/get-it-sold/show/index.html

- *House Doctor – Home Staging Makeover Show*
  www.housedoctor.co.uk/tv-series/index.php

- *Mission: Organization – Home Organization Makeover Show*
  www.hgtv.com/mission-organization/show/index.html

- *Secrets That Sell*
  www.hgtv.com/secrets-that-sell/show/index.html

- *Sell This House – Home Staging Makeover Show*
  www.aetv.com/sell_this_house/sell_about.jsp

- *The Stagers*
  www.hgtv.com/the-stagers/show/index.html

- *The Unsellables*
  www.hgtv.com/the-unsellables/show/index.html

3.5.2 Books

Invest in a personal library of design books which will serve as a reference for inspiration and industry information as your business grows.

If you are on a shoe-string budget, visit your local public library and check out a few books on decorating topics.

For those who have not completed formal training in interior design, reading a book that covers design fundamentals, architecture, and the history of style will be beneficial in forming your creative foundation. Along with books on interior design and decorating theory, there are also books tailored to home staging concepts. A few books you may want to read include:

- *Decorating for Good: A Step-by-Step Guide to Rearranging What You Already Own,*
  by Carole Talbott

- *Doghouse to Dollhouse for Dollars,*
  by Jeanette Fisher

- *Dress Your House for Success,*
  by Martha Webb and Sarah Parsons Zackheim

- *Home Staging: The Winning Way to Sell Your House for More Money,*
  by Barb Schwarz

- *How to Increase the Value of Your Home: Simple, Budget-Conscious Techniques and Ideas That Will Make Your Home Worth Up to $100,000 More!*
  by Vicki Lankarge

- *Improve the Value of Your Home up to $100,000: 50 Sure-Fire Techniques and Strategies,*
  by Robert Irwin

- *Interior Design Course: Principles, Practices, and Techniques for the Aspiring Designer,*
  by Tomris Tangaz

- *Room Redux: The Home Decorating Workbook,*
  by Joann Eckstut

- *The Beverly Hills Organizer's Home Organizing Bible: A Pro's Answers to Your Organizing Prayers,* by Linda Koopersmith

- *Use What You Have Decorating,* by Lauri Ward

3.5.3 Magazines

Design magazines are terrific resources because they deliver fresh, new products and ideas on a recurring monthly basis. These photo-filled publications will keep you ahead of style and color trends, and you will also get acquainted with the leading suppliers and manufacturers in the design industry. Look for copies of the following magazines at a bookstore, newsstand, or library, so that you can test the waters before diving into a subscription:

- *Interior Design*
  With a focus on the interior design profession, this visually spectacular magazine also showcases the finest designer work.
  www.interiordesign.net

- *Architectural Digest*
  Because it's loaded with photographs of the world's most stunning homes, this is a top interior design magazine.
  www.architecturaldigest.com

- *House Beautiful*
  An eclectic decorating magazine with ideas and product reviews for all budget levels.
  www.housebeautiful.com

- *Dwell Magazine*
  Surveys modern home design both inside and out.
  www.dwell.com

- *Better Homes and Gardens*
  A variety of articles about interior and exterior decorating and home improvement. Also features a subscription-based Decorating Toolbox.
  www.bhg.com

- *Elle Décor*
  A home fashion magazine with an international flavor.
  www.elledecor.com

- *Metropolitan Home*
  When it comes to the newest design trends and products, this publication continues to beat the crowd while exhibiting the work of the world's preeminent designers.
  www.methome.com

3.5.4 Online Resources

- *Visual Coordinations*
  www.ctalbott.com

- *Use What You Have - Lauri Ward*
  www.redecorate.com

- *Bassett Furniture – Room Designer*
  www.bassettfurniture.com/tools/room-planner.asp

- *Coldwell Banker Realty – Open House Seller Checklist*
  www.coldwellbanker.com/real_estate/Seller_Resources

- *HGTV Home Organizing Tips*
  www.hgtv.com/topics/organization/index.html

- *Home Organizing Articles*
  www.essortment.com/in/Home.Organizing/index.htm

As you explore the Internet, you will come across a bounty of interior decorating websites which contain innovative ideas, designer makeovers, and solutions for almost any room challenge. These wide-ranging online reference tools are a tremendous source to tap into, thanks to daily updates featured on the majority of sites. Some of the best interior decorating websites for valuable content and truly useful information include Home & Garden Television (**www.hgtv.com**), GetDecorating.com (**www.getdecorating.com**), and Better Homes and Gardens (**www.bhg.com/decorating**). You can get tips from Martha Stewart Living by visiting **www.marthastewart.com** (click on "Home & Garden").

4. Starting Your Own Business

Being armed with the knowledge of how to stage a home is only half the battle. You will need to be equally prepared to start and run a successful, thriving business.

While you should spend considerable time thinking about and planning your business launch, Debra Gould, The Staging Diva®, advises new stagers to "be prepared to 'learn in action' and don't hide at home waiting for everything to be perfect before you start." This chapter will explain how easy it can be to start a new company, when you know what to focus on and what to avoid.

4.1 Getting Started

4.1.1 Creating a Business Plan

Ultimately, it's your decision how detailed to make your business plan or if you even draft one at all. At a minimum, I advise putting together an uncomplicated plan that outlines your business goals and marketing strategy. This puts you on the path to being profitable and provides an action plan for growing your business.

Your trek from week to week will be easier with your eyes wide open, knowing where your company is headed. Most importantly, a business plan will give you confidence as you make financial decisions that support both your immediate and long-term ambitions. Cheryl Clifford of A New View says, "I did write a business plan when I started, but you must revisit the plan at least yearly."

One factor that will determine how meticulous your business plan should be is your need for outside investors. If you are financing the start-up yourself, then the plan will be more for your own personal goal setting, and a less in-depth plan should work. If you will require investors or loans, then a fully functioning plan should be drafted in order to secure your funding.

There are several types of business plans to consider:

- *Starter Plan:* This miniature business plan covers just the essentials and can be your starting point for a more detailed plan in the future. Use a starter plan to forecast your potential income and see how many clients will be needed to reach that goal. Then outline how you will get those clients.
- *Functional Plan:* This is a working model for everyday business operations. Since it will be for your eyes only, this more comprehensive plan doesn't have to look pretty, but it should thoroughly cover all the major financial and marketing issues.
- *Investor Plan:* This is basically a more professional, polished version of the functional business plan which can be shown to loan officers or potential backers. This plan contains projections on how and when you can pay back any loans.

Parts of a Plan

Because of the research and calculations involved, writing a business plan will answer a lot of questions you may have about starting a home staging company. A meaningful plan will describe your goals and layout your strategies to meet those goals. Review your plan often and make the necessary adjustments as your company changes.

The basic components of a functional business plan include:

Your Business Concept

This section should explain the overall industry, the services to be offered, the legal business structure, and your basic map for success.

Market Analysis

The best way to cover all your bases here is to conduct a situational or SWOT analysis (Strengths, Weaknesses, Opportunities, and Threats):

- What are your company's strengths, or what is done well?
- What are the weaknesses, or what can be improved upon?
- What are your business opportunities? Determine your immediate target market and note any emerging prospects.
- What are the threats to your company? List your competitors and economic factors that could pose a challenge for this type of business.

Marketing Plan

After completing a situational analysis, you should now specify your plan for implementing the marketing mix, also known as the four P's of marketing (product, price, place, and promotion):

- Detail the products or services you will sell and why they are beneficial to your clients. List any differential advantage you may have over the competition.
- Conduct market research to determine the best pricing strategy for your services.
- List the place, or when and where, your services will be distributed. As a home stager, this is usually the client's residence.
- Describe your promotional plan to reach your target market. This should include advertising tactics, public relations efforts, and

your personal selling strategies. Mention your plans to track and evaluate all promotional activity to see what attracted the most clients.

Financials

In this section, you should explain the need for any capital, plot your income or cash flow projections, and map your break-even points. You should also list your start-up budget and an operating budget for the first year. A profit-and-loss statement should expand your break-even numbers across several months or a year. Much of your data will come from educated guesses based on assumptions, so be sure to clarify your rationale.

Management and Operations

This is a chance to describe how your specific background relates to the business. Discuss the daily operating activities that you will pursue. Also, go over your organizational structure if you will have any employees or plan to in the future.

Small Business Planning Resources

Crafting a functional business plan might appear to be a daunting task, but there are plenty of available tools to help entrepreneurs soar effortlessly through the process. Community colleges and local universities often feature low-cost continuing education classes that focus on entrepreneurship or starting a business. Call your local Chamber of Commerce to locate a business assistance center which specializes in helping start-ups, often for little to no cost.

Look into these other resources for expert help with your business endeavors:

- *Canada Business – Interactive Business Planner*
  www.canadabusiness.ca/ibp/en/

- *Entrepreneur Magazine*
  (Business plan information and sample plans)
  www.entrepreneur.com/businessplan

- Nolo
  (Click on "Business & Human Resources,"
  then on "Starting a Business")
  www.nolo.com

- *Palo Alto Software – Business Plan Pro*
  www.paloalto.com/business_planning.cfm

- *SCORE – Business Tools and Online Workshops*
  www.score.org/business_toolbox.html

- *The Wall Street Journal – MiniPlan Building Tool*
  (Free registration required)
  http://wsj.miniplan.com

4.1.2 Choosing a Legal Structure

All businesses, even those run by one person, must designate a legal structure for their operation. Even though you will most likely function as a sole proprietorship, there a several options outlined below for you to consider. Many entrepreneurs find it easier and less complex to work as a sole proprietor in the beginning and then reevaluate their business structure later on down the road.

Sole Proprietorship

This straightforward business structure makes you the legal equivalent to your business. Money made from the company is lumped into your personal income taxes with the filing of a Schedule C form. Also, you may be required to make estimated tax payments each quarter to offset your final income tax bill and pay the social security tax. One downside is that this type of legal structure does not protect your personal assets if there are any claims against the business.

Partnership

This is another commonly seen business structure which consists of two or more people who oversee the company, sharing both the profits and the liabilities. In a general partnership, each partner has an agreed upon percentage of responsibility for all aspects of the business and reports earnings as personal income. As an alternative, the limited partnership features silent partners who aren't daily participants in the business and who are only liable up to their investment amount. It would be worthwhile to have a written partnership agreement drawn up with the help of a legal professional.

Corporation

At some point, you may want to think about incorporating your company to protect your personal assets from liabilities and legal claims. Corporations are business entities separate from any person involved with the company.

This type of legal structure is established when a business incorporates, and shares in the corporation are then sold to investors or shareholders. A lot of official procedures are involved, such as annual reports which will be requested when the corporation's taxes are paid. Small businesses may benefit from setting up a subchapter S corporation which provides personal liability protection and avoids double taxation, since business profits are given directly to shareholders as personal income.

Limited Liability Company

An LLC business structure gives you the benefits of a partnership or S corporation while providing personal asset protection like a corporation. Similar to incorporating, there will be substantial paperwork involved in establishing this business structure. LLCs have flexible tax options, but are usually taxed like a partnership.

If you decide to organize your business as a corporation, limited partnership, or LLC, additional legal requirements for the business name may call for a professional search by a lawyer, in order to ensure a unique name within your state of operation. This search will make certain that your business name receives trademark protection. You can also contact the state filing office and ask to search their database. In addition, you can explore the online database of the U.S. Patent and Trademark Office (**www.uspto.gov/main/trademarks.htm**). Or if you wish, there are online legal services like **www.legalzoom.com** which will perform a trademark search.

For more information on business structures, you can take a look at the resources available through FindLaw at **http://smallbusiness.findlaw.com/business-structures**.

4.1.3 Naming Your Business

There are a few things to consider when deciding how to name your business. Your business name needs to:

- Describe what you do
- Be easy to pronounce
- Attract customers
- Be unique
- Be available

To choose a name for your home staging company, start by taking a look in the phone book or on the Internet to see the names that other home stagers have chosen. Notice which names stand out. When you've decided on a few names that sound fabulous, let some friends and colleagues know what you're thinking of calling your business, and ask for their comments and opinions. The decision is still up to you, of course, but the instant reactions of "real people" can be a good indication of whether you are on the right track or not.

Here are name samples from the home staging business owners we surveyed.

- A Perfect Placement
- Center Stage Home
- Enhanced Equity Home Staging
- Prepared to Sell
- Stage to Sell
- Stageffect, Inc.
- The Staging Diva®

In most jurisdictions, once you have chosen your business name you will also have to file a "Doing Business As" (DBA) application, to register the fictitious name under which you will conduct your business operations. The DBA allows you to operate under a name other than your own legal name.

Filing a DBA usually takes place at the county level, although some states require that you file at the state level, publish your intent to operate under an assumed business name, and sign an affidavit stating that you have done so. However, in most cases it's usually just a short form to fill out and a small filing fee that you pay to your state or provincial government. You can find links at the Business.gov website to the appropriate government departments where you can file your business name at **www.business.gov/register/business-name/dba.html**.

It's important that your business name not resemble the name of another similar business offering similar services. For one thing, prospective clients may confuse the other business with yours and go with your competitor's services instead of yours. In addition, if you do use a name too similar to another business that was in business first they will have grounds for legal action against you.

Before officially registering your business name, you must conduct formal fictitious names and trademark searches. (The fictitious names database is where non-trademarked business names are listed.) A trademark database lists all registered and trademarked business names. In the U.S., the essential place to start is with the U.S. Patent and Trademark Office. You can hire a company to do a name search for you, or conduct a free search yourself at the PTO's website at **www.uspto.gov/main/trademarks.htm**.

> **TIP:** Stagedhomes.com and Barb Schwarz hold a U.S. Federal Registered Trademark on the word "Stage" for printed marketing materials and for DVDs used in their training programs, although anyone can use the word "Stage" or "Stager" in their own home staging business.

In Canada, the default database for name searches is the Newly Upgraded Automated Name Search (NUANS) at **www.nuans.com**. There is a $20 charge for each NUANS search. You can also hire a company such as Arvic Search Services (**www.arvic.com**) or **www.bizname search.com** to help you with name searches, trademarks and incorporating your business for a fee. Check online for "corporate registry services" to find other companies.

If you would like to learn more about this subject, you can read an in-depth article about naming your business entitled "How to Name Your Business" at the Entrepreneur.com website. This article includes tips on how to brainstorm ideas for naming your business, as well as establishing trademarks and how to file a DBA. A related article, "8 Mistakes to Avoid When Naming Your Business" offers tips on avoiding some typical business naming mistakes. You can find both of these articles at **www.entrepreneur.com/startingabusiness/startupbasics/index144024.html** (click on "Naming Your Business" in the "Browse by Topic" section).

4.1.4 Franchising

After reading the previous sections, you may be wondering if there's an easier way to get your business started than to do it yourself. If you are eager to start your own business, but are concerned about the many facets involved in getting everything set up, you may want to consider franchising.

Franchising is a business model which allows someone (you) to run a local business using an established regional or national company or corporation name, logo, products, services, marketing and business systems. The original company is known as the "franchisor" and the company that is granted the right to run its business the same way as the franchisor is known as the "franchisee."

You have probably bought products and services from many franchises. McDonald's Burger King, Wendy's and many other fast-food outlets are franchises, as are many other types of businesses. Recent figures from industry analysts estimate that franchising companies and their franchisees accounted for more than $1 trillion in annual U.S. retail sales from 760,000 franchised small businesses in 75 industries, so clearly franchises can be successful business models.

Pros and Cons of Franchising

Often, people who choose to franchise do so because they want to minimize their risk. By working with an established system, franchisees hope to avoid costly mistakes and make a profit more quickly, especially since the business probably already has name recognition, products and marketing concepts that are popular among the public.

Franchising offers some unique advantages. Buying a ready-made business means you do not have to agonize over the minute details of a business plan, you do not have to create a logo and letterhead, and the organization of your store is already done. Plus, there is less risk with a ready-made business with a proven track record.

Franchises are good for people who want support running their businesses. The franchisee may receive assistance with everything from obtaining supplies to setting up record keeping systems. Many franchisors are continuously working to develop better systems and products and you can take advantage of those developments. Franchisors typically provide a complete business plan for managing and operating the establishment. The plan provides step-by-step procedures for major aspects of the business and provides a complete matrix for the management decisions confronted by its franchisees.

If you choose to franchise, remember that although you own the store you do not own any of the trademarks or business systems. A franchisee must run their business according to the terms of their agreement with the franchisor. In exchange for the security, training, and marketing power of the franchise trademark, you must be willing to give up some of your independence. If you are a person who likes to make most decisions on your own or to chart the course of your business alone, a franchise may not be right for you.

Since someone else is ultimately "in charge," you may be wondering how having a franchise is different than being an employee. In fact, there are significant differences. You have more freedom than an employee; for example, you might choose your own working hours. And you could ultimately earn a lot more money than an employee.

On the other hand, franchisees must pay thousands of dollars up front for the opportunity to work with the business. In addition, you will be required to cover your own operating costs (including the cost of staffing your store to the levels required by the franchisor), pay a franchise fee and a percentage of total sales.

Costs

Entrepreneur Magazine describes a franchise fee as a one-time charge paid to the franchisor "for the privilege of using the business concept, attending their training program, and learning the entire business." Other start-up costs may include the products and services you will actually need to run the business, such as supplies, store fixtures, computer equipment, advertising, etc. The fees for operation will vary from franchise to franchise, and may rely heavily on location, but expect the franchise fee to be somewhere between $15,000-$25,000, with additional start-up costs.

There are a variety of factors involved in determining the initial investment. For example, if you are interested in operating a Showhomes franchise, the average investment will cost anywhere between $123,000 to more than $300,000 depending on the geographic location and the size of the store. (These investment figures are higher in Canada, for example.) Most franchise owners obtain financing for their business by providing approximately 35% of the total capital, and then arrange a business loan from a local bank for the balance of the total investment required. (See section 5.2.2 for more information on start-up funding.)

In addition to your initial investment, you can expect to pay the franchisor ongoing royalties, generally on a monthly basis. These royalties are usually calculated as a percentage of your gross monthly sales, and typically range from 2 percent to as much as 10 percent; the exact amount will depend on the company you franchise with. This is the corporation's cut for providing you with their business model and good name.

Choosing a Home Staging Franchise

It is important to do your homework on the company you are interested in franchising with — gather all the information you need to make an informed decision. Get some professional opinions on any franchise opportunity you're interested in. Work with an attorney who understands the laws associated with franchising. Also, you may want to work with an accountant to examine your anticipated expenses, your financing needs, and your prospects for achieving your desired level of profitability before you sign any agreement. Speak with other people who have invested in the company you are investigating and have an attorney examine the franchisor's contract.

Key points to research:

- The type of experience required in the franchised business
- Hours and personal commitment necessary to run the business
- Background of the franchisor or corporation
- Success rate of other franchisees in the same system
- Franchising fees to open the franchise
- Initial total investment required to open the franchise
- Cost of operation to continue the right to operate the business as a franchisee
- Any additional fees, products or services, such as advertising, that you must buy from the franchisor and how they are supplied

For excellent advice on franchising, visit the following websites:

- *Canadian Franchise Association*
  www.cfa.ca
- *Entrepreneur's Franchise Zone*
  www.entrepreneur.com/franchises/index.html
- *Small Business Administration: Buying a Franchise*
  www.sba.gov/smallbusinessplanner/start/buyafranchise

There are only a few companies offering franchise opportunities in the home staging market right now. Here are a couple of franchises for you to consider. Please note that the companies listed here do not represent our endorsement of these businesses. They are provided for information purposes only. Only you know which franchise, if any, is right for you.

Showhomes

Showhomes is probably the best known home staging franchisor. It has 33 franchisees across the U.S. Services offered include home staging, home redesign, and home management. They offer extensive support to franchisees, including a business mentor, custom software, marketing programs, etc.

Address:	2110 Blair Blvd Nashville, TN 37212
Phone:	615-292-0892
Website:	**www.showhomesfranchise.com**
Franchise fee:	\$75,000-\$175,000
Royalty Fee:	10%
Total Investment:	\$123,000-\$326,000

LewisStyle

LewisStyle is new in the world of home staging franchises. The company offers home staging and interior redesign services. To franchisees, the company offers an intensive 4-day training program at its corporate headquarters in Denver, Colorado, as well as ongoing support and training.

Address:	PO Box 630076 Littleton, CO 80163
Phone:	877-627-2711
Website:	**http://lewisstyle.com**
Start-up Cost:	\$12,500 to \$49,000
Total Investment:	\$12,500 to \$49,000

4.1.5 Choosing Your Location

Before you can decide where to locate your business, you have to determine what functions you need your office to serve. Take into consideration the services you provide and what tasks you will need to do in your office. Consider whether you will meet with clients at your office. Many home stagers don't, and always travel to the client's home or place of business. You will also need to consider if you have enough space to store documents and other materials, and space for future employees or partners to work.

Much like choosing a business name, your choice of office location may depend on client perception. However, if you don't intend to invite clients to your office, then a home office is the most economical place for you to establish your business. Many home stagers choose to keep their office in their home for the long term.

Working from Home

For many people, the biggest benefit of working from home is the end of the commuter lifestyle, greater freedom, and the ability to spend time with family. Another benefit for eligible businesses is that you can deduct from your income taxes a percent of your mortgage payment and property taxes (or rent) and a share of utilities and maintenance costs.

There are various methods to make those calculations, but by far the easiest – and most acceptable to the IRS – is to use an entire room, and to use it for no other purpose. In the U.S., IRS Publication 587 has information on how to compute the calculation and file the deduction. You can download this information by visiting the IRS website and searching for the publication numbers from the search engine on the front page. At the time of publication of this guide it was available online at **www.irs.gov/pub/irs-pdf/p587.pdf**.

The other thing you should check before deciding on an office at home is local zoning. Most places won't have a problem with a home-based business that adds only a few cars a day to the automobile load on your street. Most will, however, prohibit you from posting a sign in your front yard, which is okay anyway, as you will not get any clients from drive-by traffic. To find out the rules in your area, look up "zoning" or "planning" in the local government section of your phone book.

In addition to any legalities, working from home requires some planning with family members. Set regular office hours that you will insist on, both for your own focus and to keep family members from intruding when you need to work. It will be tempting for the family to interrupt you. So make it clear you are at work unless it's an emergency.

(The garage on fire is an emergency; needing to know where the cookies are is not.)

Office Space

While a home office works well for many home stagers, others prefer to rent a separate space. If you find it challenging to stay motivated, or tend to get easily distracted when you're at home, an office may be just what you need to help you focus on business. A separate space also creates a better impression if you plan to have people visit you. If you want a place to meet with clients, or work with employees, you might want to consider getting an office outside your home.

If you decide to rent space, start by determining what your requirements are. Look for a place that is convenient to get to from your home, and that gives you quick access to any services you may need. You can use the checklist below as a starting point.

If you want the appearance of a professional office space, but cost is an issue, consider shared office space in a business center or executive suite. These facilities are typically furnished offices that provide you with receptionist and mail services. They may also offer photocopiers, fax machines, Internet access, and conference rooms that you can use for client meetings. Check the Yellow Pages under "office space" or do a Google search for your city and "shared office space," "business center" or "executive suite."

Following are checklists of typical office equipment and supplies required for a home staging business. For details about the specific tools and supplies you'll need to do staging projects, and where to get them, see section 2.2. Most of the large retail office supply chains can set you up with everything you need for your office at a reasonable price.

- *Staples*
  www.staples.com

- *Office Depot*
  www.officedepot.com

- *OfficeMax*
  www.officemax.com

Office Space Checklist

Will this be an easy commute for me? *(You don't want to have to battle traffic to and from work every day if you can avoid it.)*	❑ Yes ❑ No
Is the neighborhood or district safe? *(You want to feel comfortable in your office and you want this for your clients as well.)*	❑ Yes ❑ No
Is the parking area lit well? *(Drive by at night and look at the lighting. You don't want to have to walk to your car in the dark.)*	❑ Yes ❑ No
Is there space for growth? *(You don't want to have to move to a bigger office next year.)*	❑ Yes ❑ No
Can I afford it? *(You'll want to read your lease agreement carefully, and crunch some numbers in your budget before you agree.)*	❑ Yes ❑ No

Office Furniture and Equipment Checklist

- ❑ Bookcases for reference material
- ❑ Chair(s)
- ❑ Computer and software
- ❑ Printer/fax/copier/scanner
- ❑ Desk (one or more)
- ❑ Filing cabinet
- ❑ Lamps and lighting
- ❑ Storage shelves
- ❑ Work table

Supplies and Small Equipment Checklist

- ❑ Accordion files
- ❑ Binders
- ❑ Brochures
- ❑ Business cards
- ❑ Business stationery
- ❑ Calculator
- ❑ Cell phone
- ❑ Day planner or PDA
- ❑ Envelopes (all sizes)
- ❑ File folders
- ❑ File labels
- ❑ Index cards
- ❑ Mailing labels
- ❑ Mailing envelopes
- ❑ Paper
- ❑ Paper clips
- ❑ Paper cutter *(for trimming brochures, postcards, etc.)*
- ❑ Pens, pencils, markers, and erasers
- ❑ Post-it notes
- ❑ Postage stamps
- ❑ Rubber bands
- ❑ Ruler
- ❑ Stapler and staples
- ❑ Tape

4.2 Financial Matters

4.2.1 Start-Up Costs and Operating Expenses

The initial start-up budget is one component of your business plan that you will want to create first. After you calculate this amount, you'll know if there's any need for investors or loans. A major benefit to working in this field is the low amount needed to get the ball rolling. In general, service businesses are cheaper to launch than businesses that sell products, because there is no inventory to buy or retail location to open.

Debra Gould of Six Elements Inc. reveals, "I didn't have expenses other than a cell phone and business cards. I built my own website and found ways to get others to promote me. I did however put many, many hours into it." If your budget is tight, it's entirely possible that this approach could work for you.

If you have significant money to invest upfront, you could buy furniture or props to use on projects. A budget-friendly option to buying staging inventory is to have your clients rent any furniture that is needed, until you can establish partnerships with furniture vendors or build up your own inventory.

As discussed in Chapter 3, a training program or workshop can have its rewards, but it will also have an enrollment fee. Lauren Bartel of New Dawn Décor says her biggest start-up expense was training: "To gain some practical experience, I chose to take a five day hands-on interior redesign course which cost $2,500." If you decide that a home staging course is the right path for you, be sure to include tuition and other training related costs in your start-up budget.

Expenses to Expect

Let's take a look at the foreseeable costs involved in launching your business, so that you can quickly and easily calculate your start-up budget. I recommend keeping your initial expenses as lean as possible. After you have some cash flow from a few staging jobs, you can buy the extras that were not in the original budget.

Here are the basic needs and expenses to anticipate:

- *Phone system:* This can be a traditional landline telephone or a cell phone, but it should be devoted solely to business use. That way, you can professionally answer your phone with your company greeting. Another must-have item is an answering machine or voicemail, so that your clients can leave a message if you're busy.

- *Cards and letterhead:* The most important thing you'll need is a box of business cards. This little billboard will be indispensable as you market yourself. It provides an immediate acknowledgment of your business to clients, vendors, and contractors. Another vital item is a box of blank cards for writing thank you notes. After client meetings or networking events, send a thank-you note along with a few business cards. You may also want some company letterhead for business correspondence or thank-you letters. To save money, create your own letterhead with a word processing program by inserting your logo into a letter template.

- *Office set-up:* Even though you will presumably be working from home, there is still a need for a comfortable place to do paperwork and conduct other business activities.

- *Camera:* A simple film-loaded camera might do, but a digital camera is preferred because it allows you to immediately download photos of your work into the computer. Building a portfolio of before and after photos will be instrumental in winning more clients.

- *Computer or laptop:* If you have an existing personal computer at home, this should work fine for your purposes. One advantage to a laptop is that you can bring it with you on appointments to show a digital slideshow of your portfolio or customize a proposal on the spot. The main reason to have computer access at home is for email capability. Your website or business card should feature your email address so that potential clients can easily contact you.

- *Computer software:* Basic word processing and spreadsheet applications will be adequate for most of your projects, and they may have even been installed on your computer by the manufacturer. You can add some interior design software or accounting software if you feel the need for more fire power in these two areas.

- *Printer and fax machine:* You will need some way to print client contracts, proposals, and other business documents so they're quickly at your fingertips. An affordable inkjet printer will be sufficient for this purpose, but a laser printer will print faster and more cleanly. A fax machine is also a must for corresponding with vendors, contractors, and clients. A smart solution here is the multi-function machine that is a printer, fax, copier and scanner. The copier and scanner functions will be very useful in this line of work.

- *Marketing and advertising:* This includes building and hosting your website, networking costs to attend luncheons or meetings, and any paid advertising activity. If you have the funds for it, you might consider budgeting for a small ad in your local newspaper or postcard mailings to get the word out. If you decide to run any printed advertisements, make sure you invest in a series of ads that are published about four to seven times in the chosen publication. Repetition is imperative in advertising. However, your best results will probably come from low-cost efforts like public relations, networking, and client referrals.

- *Business licenses:* You'll need to comply with any local, state, or federal requirements for operating a business in your area. This will likely involve licenses and permits for you or your contractors. While the fees shouldn't be too hefty, they should be added to the start-up budget.

- *Legal or accounting fees:* If you will need the counsel of an attorney, accountant, or bookkeeper, this expenditure should be estimated and taken into account. Professional services are an area where expenses can be higher than expected, so do your research and try to work out flat fee arrangements.

- *Insurance:* While not usually mandatory in this industry, general liability insurance for your business can provide peace of mind while working on your clients' property. Find out if this is legally required in your area for your type of business. You can also protect yourself by making sure all subcontractors you hire are insured and bonded. You may also need to add in costs for health insurance or disability insurance, if you need these policies.

- *Living expenses:* Since you won't have a steady paycheck as an entrepreneur, it is crucial that you save up about three to six months worth of living expenses; especially if you have no other sources of income to drawn on while you build your business.
- *Training:* Any programs or workshops in which you enroll should be added into the budget. In many cases, training may end up being one of the top expenses. There are also small business classes or continuing education classes that you may decide to take.
- *Office supplies:* These items aren't expensive on their own, but it can add up fast if you don't keep tabs on it. Stick to the basics and refer to the office supply list in section 4.1.5. One necessity is a supply of file folders to keep track of client contracts and project notes.

A start-up worksheet has been included on the next page to simplify the process. Once you've researched how much each item will cost, fill in those amounts and total up your starting budget. The overall amount will largely depend on what items you already own.

Monthly Operating Expenses

Your monthly operating expenses include both fixed and variable costs. Fixed costs remain the same from month to month regardless of the amount of work you do (examples include rent and membership dues), while variable costs may vary from month to month (examples include travel and taxes). To estimate monthly variable costs, start by estimating a yearly total than divide that by 12 for a monthly average.

Creating a monthly budget will help you plan for your first year in business. After the first year, you can then build a budget for year two based on what you actually spent during your first year. Your monthly budget will also help you determine what costs you need to cover before you start making a profit.

Your own costs may vary widely from those of other home stagers, depending on what you currently have and what you plan to do with your business. For example, your rent might range from $0 if you have a home office to $1,000 per month for leased office space.

Start-Up Expenses

Item	Cost	Item	Cost
Office furniture (see checklist in this section)	_______	Digital Camera	_______
		Stationery	_______
Computer	_______	Business cards	_______
Printer/copier/fax/ scanner (separate or all-in-one)	_______	Printing (brochures or other marketing materials)	_______
Office software	_______	Website setup costs (design, domain name, etc.)	_______
Business phone line installation fee	_______	Business licenses/fees	_______
Telephone	_______	Professional consulting (lawyer, accountant)	_______
Office supplies	_______	Other (list each item)	_______
		TOTAL:	_______

Monthly Operating Expenses

Item	Cost	Item	Cost
Salaries	_______	Printing materials	_______
Benefits	_______	Marketing expenses	_______
Rent (or portion of mortgage)	_______	Web hosting	_______
Office supplies (see checklist later in this section)	_______	Magazine subscriptions and professional literature	_______
Telephone	_______	Training and conferences	_______
Internet service	_______	Legal and accounting services	_______
Postage and courier	_______	Banking expenses	_______
Travel expenses including mileage	_______	Entertainment	_______
Insurance costs	_______	Taxes	_______
Membership dues	_______	Other (list each item)	_______
		TOTAL:	_______

Keeping Track of Your Finances

Here are some tactics to use to keep track of your business income and expenses. First, open a business account at a bank, trust company or credit union, even if you are using only your own name to do business. Use this only for paying the bills of the company and your own salary, which you then deposit in your personal account.

Get a style of business check that requires you to record checks you've written. You want to create a paper trail for your business account so you are able to:

- Prove your deductions at tax time
- See at a glance where your money has gone
- Create balance sheets that your vendors or other financial institutions may request from time to time

Also, keep track of your accounts receivable, accounts payable, and so on in a ledger book, which you can get at any office supply store. Or else use an electronic bookkeeping package. The most popular bookkeeping software for small businesses is Quicken (**http://quicken.intuit.com**). For under a hundred dollars, Quicken's Home and Business program will help you prepare invoices, manage your accounts, and generate reports from your records.

Finally, keep two additional ledgers – small enough to carry in your purse or briefcase – so you can log (1) mileage (or other travel expenses), and (2) everything you spend during the day (remember to keep personal and business expenses separate).

Also carry an envelope so you can keep receipts for everything you buy. The cup of coffee you buy for a prospective customer, the latest issue of a business magazine, the mileage you travel to a client's office, the pack of paper you pick up at the office supply store, the admission charge for a trade fair — these and many other expenses should be accounted for so you can minimize your taxes. And, of course, knowing exactly where your money is going will help you plan better and cut back on any unnecessary expenses. So make it a habit to ask for a receipt for every expense related to business.

Be sure to re-file these at night in the appropriate files in your file cabinet. The business receipts should be stapled to the order form for each purchase/service for a client. No matter how you design a system, make sure it works for you and that you can find receipts for anything at any time.

4.2.2 Start-Up Financing

Although the start-up costs for starting a home staging business are minimal, you may want to secure a loan or investment to get through the early months, purchase some office equipment, or lease office space.

In business, there are two basic kinds of financing: equity financing and debt financing. The decision to choose debt or equity financing usually will be based on your personal financial position and how much additional money you need in order to get your business started. Essentially, equity financing is when you agree to give someone a share in your business in exchange for an agreed amount of investment capital from that person.

Debt financing is any form of borrowing money, including a loan, lease, line of credit or other debt on which you must pay interest in order to finance the original principal amount. Sources for this kind of financing include banks, credit unions, credit card companies, suppliers, and so on. If you buy a computer system for your company and pay for it in monthly installments over a couple of years, that is a form of debt financing since you will pay interest on the amount you finance. Consider all your options carefully and, especially before you enter into any kind of long-term debt arrangement, speak with an accountant and a lawyer first.

Only you can decide which financing sources will be the best ones for your business and your personal situation. The most important thing is to make sure you agree to loan repayment terms that you can live with and that are realistic for you. In the following sections we'll look at some of the sources of each type of financing and the advantages and disadvantages to each. Additional advice on all aspects of financing your business can be found at the SBA's Small Business Planner website at **www.sba.gov** (under "Start Your Business", click on "Finance Start-Up" then choose "Financing Basics"). In Canada, visit **http://bsa.canadabusiness.ca/gol/bsa/site.nsf/en/su04919.html**.

TIP: Many financial consultants recommend having a nest egg to live on while you are starting up your business. Some suggest at least six months' of living expense money — that is, all the money you will need monthly to pay all your personal living expenses, bills, and debts, so you can focus on your new business without stress. This is apart from any start-up capital you might need for the business itself.

Commercial Loans

Commercial loans are loans that you can get from a financial institution. These include traditional banks, credit unions, savings and loans and commercial finance companies. The terms of your loan will depend upon several things, including your credit score, your collateral, and your ability to pay back a loan. Be sure to compare interest rates and terms of lending to see which institution offers the best deals.

When you are starting your business, financial institutions will likely lend the money to you personally rather than to your business, as a result, they are much more interested in your personal financial status than your business plan. A business just starting up won't count as collateral, so you'll probably need to guarantee the loan with personal assets like your house or your car.

They will look at how much money you need every month to pay your bills, what kind of resources or assets you have, what kind of debt you are in, and how you will repay this debt.

In that case, the lending institution will insist on seeing a formal business plan that demonstrates clearly-defined financial and business goals. (If you haven't read it already, see section 4.1.1 for advice on creating a business plan.) You will also need to prepare a loan proposal, which includes a credit application, and provide information about your business including the following:

- The type of loan you're applying for
- Amount you are requesting
- What you will use for collateral
- How the money will be used

- Information about your business, its name, legal structure, tax numbers, existing loans, taxes owed, assets
- Details about the business owners or principals: name, mortgages, source of other income

Family and Friends

One of the greatest resources for your start-up money will always be the people you know who believe in you and your ideas—your family and friends. Very often they will help you with money when all other resources fail you. They usually will agree to payback terms that aren't as strict as commercial lenders, and they are usually pulling for you, too. As with any other kind of loan, it is important to make sure that you and the other parties completely understand and agree to the terms of the loan. Make sure you have a written document which states when and how you will pay the loan back.

Another possibility is to ask a family member to co-sign a commercial loan for you. Co-signing means that this person agrees to take on the financial responsibility of the loan if you should fail. Family members are often willing to help you out this way. Make sure, before friends or family members help you out by co-signing a loan, that they are really comfortable doing so.

Partners

One of the simplest forms of equity financing is taking on a partner. Having a partner in your business brings additional skill sets, business contacts and resources to the venture. Most importantly, a partner can bring money to help pay for start-up costs and assist with ongoing operations. You'll need to decide whether your partner will be active in the running of the company or just a silent partner who invests the money, receives income from the business, but has no say in how things are run. (You can read more about Partnerships as a form of business legal structure in section 4.1.2)

You as an Investor

Never forget that you might be your own best source of funding. One nice thing about using your own money is that you aren't obligated to anyone else or any other organization—it is yours to invest. This can be an excellent solution for individuals with some credit problems.

To raise your own capital, you can:

- Cash out stocks, bonds, life insurance, an IRA, RRSP, or other retirement account
- Increase your credit on charge cards (remember that you will pay high interest rates on these)
- Use personal savings
- Take out a second mortgage or home equity loan on your house or other property
- Sell something valuable, like a car, jewelry, real estate, or art

Government Programs

Small Business Administration Loans

The Small Business Administration (SBA) doesn't actually lend you money. However, they have a program called the "7(a) Loan Program" in which they work with banks to provide loan services to small business owners. The SBA guarantees a percentage of the loan that a commercial lender will give you, so that if you default on your payments, the bank will still get back the amount guaranteed by the SBA. As the borrower, you are still responsible for the full amount of the loan. When you apply for a small business loan, you will actually apply at your local bank. The bank then decides whether they will make the loan internally or use the SBA program.

The SBA also provides a pre-qualification program that assists business start-ups in putting together a viable funding request package for submission to lenders. They will work with you to help you apply for a loan up to a maximum amount of $250,000. Once the loan package has been submitted, studied, and approved by the SBA, they will issue a commitment letter on your behalf that you can submit to lenders for consideration. They provide the extra assurance that many lenders need to get entrepreneurs the financing they need. You can read more about the process at **www.sba.gov** (click on "Services" then on "Financial Assistance").

Another program offered by the SBA is a "Micro-Loans" program, which offers loans to start-up and newly established businesses through non-profit entities at the local level up to a maximum of $35,000. The average loan is about $13,000. Interest rates for these small loans vary between about 8 to 13 percent. You can find out more about these loans at the SBA website.

Government Programs in Canada

If you are planning to open a retail business in Canada, you might be interested in the Business Development Bank of Canada (BDC) or the Canada Small Business Financing Program (CSBF). The BDC is a financial institution owned by the federal government that offers consulting and financing services to help get small businesses started. They also have a financing program aimed specifically at women entrepreneurs. You can learn more about the Business Development Bank of Canada (BDC) and its financing resources at **www.bdc.ca**.

The Canada Small Business Financing Program is much like the SBA 7(a) Loan Program mentioned earlier in this section. The maximum amount you can borrow is $250,000, and the funds must be used to purchase real property, leasehold improvements or equipment. The CSBFP works with lenders across the country to offer loans at 3% above the lender's prime lending rate. To find out more, visit **www.ic.gc.ca/eic/site/csbfp-pfpec.nsf/eng/la00049.html**.

4.2.3 Taxes

Why can't everything be as fun as staging a house? Being a small business owner means that inevitably you have to deal with sticky subjects like paying your taxes and filing government paperwork. While these activities might be uninspiring, the rewards of working for yourself will motivate you to supersede these mundane activities.

If you are properly informed and prepared you won't have to face your tax responsibility with a feeling of dread. In fact, once you are organized and you have enlisted the help of a good tax professional, taxes become just another regular business task.

Get Informed First

The best thing you can do to be sure of your personal and business tax obligations is to find the information you need before you start your new business. The Internal Revenue Service (IRS) has a number of informative documents online that you can look at today to learn the basics about everything you need to prepare for your taxes as a small business owner. If you read these documents and understand them, you will have no surprises at tax time.

One helpful document is the *Tax Guide for Small Businesses* that outlines your rights and responsibilities as a small business owner. It tells you how to file your taxes, and provides an overview of the tax system for small businesses. You can find this document at **www.irs.gov/pub/irs-pdf/p334.pdf**. For more general information for small business owners from the IRS visit their website at **www.irs.gov/businesses/small/index.html**.

For Canadian residents, the Canada Revenue Agency also provides basic tax information for new business owners. This includes information about the GST, how to file your taxes, allowable expenses and so on. You can find this information and more helpful documents at **www.cra-arc.gc.ca/tx/bsnss/menu-eng.html**.

It is also important to be informed about your tax obligations on a state and local level. Tax laws and requirements vary on a state-by-state basis and locally, too. Make sure that you find out exactly what you are responsible for in your state and city. In addition, it is important to find out about sales tax in your area. Bankrate.com provides state-by-state information on personal, sales and other taxes. Click on the "Taxes" tab at the top of their homepage, then click on "Tax Basics" or use the state directory at **www.bankrate.com/brm/itax/state/state_tax_home.asp**. The Canada Revenue Agency has a linked directory of government websites at **www.cra-arc.gc.ca/tx/bsnss/prv_lnks-eng.html** where you can find tax information on a province-by-province basis.

Getting Assistance

If you decide you would prefer a qualified tax professional to help you handle your taxes, you will find you are in good company. Many small business owners decide to have a professional handle their taxes. An accountant can point out deductions you might otherwise miss and save you a lot of money.

One resource that may assist you in choosing an accountant is the article "Finding an Accountant" by Kevin McDonald. It offers helpful advice for finding an accounting professional whose expertise matches your needs. The article is available at **www.bankrate.com/brm/news/advice/19990609c.asp**.

Once you've determined what your accounting needs are you may be able to find a professional accountant at the Accountant Finder website (**www.accountant-finder.com**). This site offers a clickable map of the United States with links to accountants in cities across the country. Alternatively, the Yellow Pages directory for your city is a good place to find listings for accountants.

You will also need to understand payroll taxes if you plan on hiring employees. Each new employee needs to fill out paperwork prior to their first pay check being issued. In the U.S. this will be a W-4 and an I-9 form. In Canada, the employee will have to complete a T-4 and fill out a Canada Pension form. Both the W-4 and the T-4 are legal documents verifying the tax deductions a new employee has. The amount of tax you will withhold as an employer varies and is based on the required deductions an employee has as specified by the federal government. Make sure you retain the forms in a folder labeled with their name and store them in a readily accessible place such as a filing cabinet in your office.

Check with your state or province's labor office to make sure you are clear about all the forms employees must fill out in order to work for you. The sites below give more information on legal paperwork, including where to get blank copies of the forms your employees will need to fill out.

- *Smart Legal Forms*
  (Sells employee forms online)
  www.hrlawinfo.com

- *GovDocs Employee Records and Personnel Forms*
  (Click on "Employee Records")
  www.hrdocs.com/Posters/hrproducts

- *Canada Revenue Agency*
  (Download and print any form you need)
  www.cra-arc.gc.ca/forms/

4.2.4 Insurance

Insurance can help protect the investment you make in your company from unforeseen circumstances or disaster. Types of insurance for the small business owner are listed in this section. Contact your insurance broker to determine whether these or other types of coverage are right for you.

You may also want to check out the National Association for the Self-Employed (**www.nase.org**) which offers reasonably priced insurance plans for self-employed people. State Farm has a program available specifically for home-based businesses which you can learn about at **www.statefarm.com/insurance/business/homebus.asp**.

Liability Insurance

This insurance (also known as Errors and Omissions Insurance) protects you against loss if you are sued for alleged negligence. It could pay judgments against you (up to the policy limits) along with any legal fees you incur defending yourself. For example, if you neglect to distribute a new company policy document to the company's employees, thinking that management was responsible for doing this and the company experiences financial losses as a result, you might find this type of insurance valuable.

TIP: For some small businesses, getting a Business Owner's policy is a good place to start. These policies are designed for small business owners with under one hundred employees and revenue of under one million dollars. These policies combine liability and property insurance together. Small business owners like these policies because of their convenience and affordable premiums. You can find out more about these policies at the Insurance Information Institute (**www.iii.org/insurance_topics**).

Property Insurance

This insurance covers losses to your personal property from damage or theft. If your business will be located in your home, you're most likely already covered with homeowner's insurance. However, it's a good idea to update your plan to provide coverage for office equipment and other items that aren't included in a standard plan.

If your business will be located in a building other than your home, you may need an additional policy. If you rent space, you'll need property insurance only on the equipment you have in your office — the owner of the building normally would pay for insurance on the property.

Life and Disability Insurance

If you provide a portion of your family's income, then you need to carry life insurance and disability insurance to make certain they are cared for if something happens to you. If you become sick or otherwise disabled for an extended period, your business could be in jeopardy. Disability insurance would provide at least a portion of your income while you're not able to be working.

Business Interruption Insurance

This insurance covers your bills and lost profit while you are out of operation for a covered loss, such as a fire. Just because the business is shut down doesn't mean the bills stop coming. This type of insurance covers ongoing expenses such as rent or taxes until your business gets up and running again.

Car Insurance

Be sure to ask your broker about your auto insurance if you'll be using your personal vehicle on company business.

Health Insurance

If you live in the United States and aren't covered under a spouse's health plan, you'll need to consider your health insurance options. You can compare health insurance quotes at **www.ehealthinsurance.com** which offers plans from over 150 insurance companies nationwide.

TIP: Some insurance companies offer discount pricing for members of particular organizations. When you are looking for organizations to join, whether your local Chamber of Commerce or a national association, check to see if discounted health insurance is one of the member benefits.

Canadians have most of their health care expenses covered by the Canadian government. For expenses that are not covered (such as dental care, eyeglasses, prescription drugs, etc.) self-employed professionals may get tax benefits from setting up their own private health care plan. Puhl Employee Benefits (**www.puhlemployeebenefits.com**) is an example of the type of financial planning company that can help you set up your own private health care plan.

More Information

The Small Business Administration has an excellent insurance and risk management guide for small businesses available online at **www.sba.gov/tools/resourcelibrary/publications/serv_pub_mplan.html** (scroll down to #17).

4.2.5 Setting Your Fees

Establishing the right pricing for your services will be a major determining factor in whether you are successful as the owner of a home staging business. Debra Gould of Six Elements Inc. advises those who are new to the industry to "really work on getting your pricing strategy right, and don't ever waste your time giving people free estimates. It's the quickest road to burn-out and bankruptcy."

Customers will ultimately pay for the services that they perceive are a good value for what they get in return. This does not mean they are looking for the lowest priced service out there. The price of a home staging service encompasses many intangibles for a potential client such as convenience, expert advice, time savings, and return on their investment. If a customer realizes that staging their home will help it sell for more than the asking price and sell it faster, then the costs to obtain that service are a wise investment in the eyes of the customer.

The most important thing to remember is that you will be in business to make a profit. In a nutshell, profit is what is left over after you pay all the expenses related to performing your services and running your business operation. You should first decide what level of profit you want or need to make and then compare that to your costs and expenses. After carrying out the right research, you will feel confident in your pricing strategy and know that there is a target market which will value your service offerings.

Factors to Consider

There are many issues that go into making a profit, starting with correctly setting your prices to make it happen. For one thing, you should always earn money to some extent on all your service offerings, even your consultations. This is simply because you can't stay in business long if you're giving the services away.

Here are the necessary factors to consider when you are setting your prices:

- Know your break-even point, or the price where your expenses are covered but you don't make or lose money. This is obviously the minimum price you should charge, and you will undoubtedly be priced well above your break-even point. Evaluate your break-even point regularly to see how much money you need to bring in, so that your expenses are covered on each job or for a given month.

- To calculate your break-even point, you'll need to know all the expenses involved in running your business, also called the cost of goods sold, or the cost of sales. This figure will include your expenses for labor, rental inventory, staging supplies, equipment, items purchased for resale, car expenses, marketing expenditures, and fixed overhead costs (rent, utilities, etc). First, identify the expenses in each of these areas, and then total them up to get your basic cost of sales.

- Recognize how valuable your service is and convey this benefit to your clients. By gathering local statistics on the effectiveness of home staging, you can educate your market as to why they need your service and why it is a good value for what they get in return. You can track your own clients' staged houses or consult with a real estate agent for some industry data. There are always national statistics to fall back on, such as the Coldwell Banker study mentioned earlier. If you offer a unique service that is in high demand, you can charge higher price points.

- Find out what price the market will bear by doing a survey that asks people what they are willing to pay for such a service. Start by inquiring with local real estate agents and homeowners in your own neighborhood for their opinions. You could also start off a reasonable, competitive price and then judge the market's reaction.

- It is essential that you shop the competition in order to discover their rates and the services they are offering. Real estate enhancement specialist, Diana Ezerins believes that you should "find out the going rate for a stager in your area and do not discount your prices." Another approach is to research the leading competitors in your field and price yourself slightly lower, until you are more established and have a sizeable portfolio or client base. That way, as your rank in the marketplace improves, you can increase your rates as well.

Ways to Set Your Rates

The two basic methods for determining your service rates are based on profit margins and market conditions. If you know your cost of goods sold and your break-even point, then you have the tools needed to set prices based on the desired profit margin. You can also use this approach to markup rental fees on inventory items or determine how to price a piece of furniture that you bought for a client.

While basing your rates on break-even points can make you money, the best chances for higher profit come from analyzing market conditions and responding accordingly. When using market-based data to position your prices, you should take into consideration your competition and the demand for your service.

Find out the rates your competitors are charging and use their market experience as a guide to setting your own rates, but be sure to keep your expenses low. You can research the competition's rates by phone, over the Internet, or with a consultation in your own home.

Determine the demand for staging in your area. Is it already a popular service or is it new to your market? Demand-based pricing means that you can raise your rates as demand increases for your services.

Armed with the information you need to set your rates, you can now decide what services to offer by the hour and which services to price as a flat fee. By and large, consultations are billed at an hourly rate and larger services are based on a flat rate fee structure. Until you get a better feel for the time involved with each project, it's best to charge by the hour.

Sample Prices

In the process of shopping the competition, you should have discovered the going rates for home stagers in your area. You should also take into account your break-even point, so you are making money in the process. Some decorators prefer to provide custom quotes for each project, but you may find that clients are more comfortable with published rates that don't fluctuate arbitrarily.

While fee structures will vary by market and with your level of experience, here is a general overview of sample prices in the industry:

Hourly rates	$35-$85
Consultation, initial 2-hour meeting before staging	$65-$150
Walk thru with written recommendations	$150-$350 (flat fee, two-hour process)
Staging, whole house	$950-$1,800 (could be higher or lower depending on client needs)
Redesign	$125-$350 per room or $550-$1,250 per house (depending on size)
Shopping	Hourly $25-$75, and/or 10% to 20% of sales made during the trip
Organizing	Hourly $35-$85

4.2.6 Getting Paid

Your service fees might be paid by the real estate agent or the homeowner, or a combination of the two. In either case, but especially with residential clients, you should request a deposit before beginning any work. This will let you know that they are serious, and it will give you some funds for buying supplies or paying subcontractors. The typical amounts for a deposit are one-third to one-half of the total expected bill. For consultations, shopping trips, and small projects, you should be paid in full at the end of each appointment.

After all the work in a client's house has been completed, you are now ready to invoice the client for the remainder of their contracted amount. Be sure to include sales tax and credit them for any deposits made at the start of the job. Then, print a copy and deliver it to the client.

Briefly review the information and cordially ask for the payment to be made at that time. If you will be mailing out the invoice instead, follow up beforehand to make sure the client is satisfied before they receive the bill in their mailbox. Your invoices should include a stipulation for adding a service charge or late fee to overdue accounts, such as 1% or 5% per month. A sample invoice has been included on the next page as a guide to formatting your own invoices.

Accepting Credit Cards

American Express and Discover cards set up merchant accounts nationally and internationally. MasterCard and Visa are local. To become a merchant accepting MasterCard and Visa, you will have to get accepted by a local acquirer (a financial institution like a bank licensed by the credit card company). Because yours is a new business, you may have to shop around to find one that gives you good rates (you may be charged between 1.5 and 3 percent per transaction for the service, and often an initial setup fee and perhaps ongoing fees for phone calls, postage, statements, and so on).

You might also have to provide evidence of a good personal financial record to set up an advantageous rate, at least until you've become established in your business and have a good track record for them to look at. Remember, the bank is granting you credit in this instance, "banking" on the fact that your customers will not want refunds or that you won't try to keep the money if they do.

These days, although the acquiring bank will be a local bank somewhere, it need not be in your hometown. Numerous services are available online to help you set up a merchant account. MasterCard and Visa accounts, as well as American Express and Discover, can all be set up through your local bank or by going to the websites of each of these companies.

A list of these websites is included on the next page.

Sample Invoice

Home Staging by Lola

Date: [*insert date*]

To: Mr. and Mrs. Joe Smith
123 Cherry
Mytown, California, 92111

Services	**Price**
Home staging services – whole house package	$ 1,200.00
Open House Detailing – hourly, on open house day	$ 100.00
Tax [Insert your local rate e.g. 8%]	$ 104.00
Less deposit [deduct any pre-payment]	$ (650.00)
Balance Due (please pay this amount)	**$ 754.00**

Terms:
Payable within 30 days. Late payments or NSF checks will be subject to a 5% fee on top of the balance due total.

Thank you for your business.

- *MasterCard Merchant*
  U.S.: **www.mastercard.com/us/merchant**
  Canada: **www.mastercard.com/ca/merchant/en/index.html**

- *Visa*
  U.S.: **http://usa.visa.com/merchants/merchant_resources/**
  Canada: **www.visa.ca/en/merchant/**

- *American Express*
  U.S.: **https://home.americanexpress.com/homepage/merchant_ne.shtml?**
  Canada: **www.americanexpress.com/canada/en/merchants/2-0_merchant.shtml**

- *Discover*
  www.discovernetwork.com/discovernetwork/howitworks/howitworks.html

Accepting Checks

When you accept checks, especially for large amounts, you may want to have a back-up system for getting paid if the client has insufficient funds in their checking account. One option is to ask the client for a credit card number which will be charged if the check does not clear.

You can accept checks from clients with greater assurance by using a check payment service such as TeleCheck. TeleCheck compares checks you receive with a database of over 51 million bad check records, allowing you to decide whether to accept a check from a particular client. The company also provides electronic payment services, from telephone debit card processing to electronic checks. You can find out more about TeleCheck at **www.telecheck.com**.

Collecting Payments

When it comes to collecting payments for client projects, there are several techniques that can be used with good results:

- A commonly used arrangement calls for you to bill the client for all contracted services at the end of the entire project, minus any upfront deposits. You will be responsible for paying any subcontractors that may have been used.

- You can also have clients pay subcontractors directly and then later collect a referral fee from each sub. This requires that you stay organized and know what referrals should be coming your way.

- Another process that works well is to have the subcontractor pick up the client's payment check when they complete the job and deliver it to you with their own invoice in hand.

- If your clients are paying by credit card, then the subs will not have to worry about collecting payments. Use a credit card processing plan with low fees, such as one that allows you to phone in transactions, or use an Internet-based service like PayPal (visit **www.paypal.com** and click on "Business").

There may be instances when you have trouble collecting a payment from a client. As a small business owner, you cannot afford any late or missing payments. Your first course of action should be to contact the client by phone and visit them in person. Ask your client if they will be making their payment soon, and if not, try to work out a reasonable payment plan with them.

If your client is not responding to your contact efforts after about two weeks, you will need to move to the next phase of collections. Send them a respectful letter along with another copy of the invoice by registered mail, so that you will know when they sign for it. If another week or two goes by with no response, send a final letter asking for the amount owed and notifying them of your intentions to file a small claims suit and a lien on their property by a specified date if you do not hear from them. Make sure to add on any service charges or late fees to their invoice. More than likely, this will be enough to get most people's attention.

The rare, but worst-case scenario is that a client decides not to pay their bill. If you received a deposit on the job, at least you won't be missing the whole amount. What can be done to ultimately collect the money? Your basic options are to use a collection agency, file a small claims suit, or file a lien on the client's property. Collection agencies are not generally recommended because they like to work with larger accounts and because they will ask for a substantial portion of the amount owed to cover their fees.

Filing a suit in small claims court is a commonly used technique for collecting overdue payments. Keep in mind, you'll need to file in the county where the client resides, and it may take awhile to get your case in front of a judge. Be sure to have important documents with you like the signed client contract or agreement and the records of your contact attempts. If a judge rules in your favor, the client will be ordered to pay, but it is still up to you to collect the money from them. In the event that the client still does not clear their account, you can then file it on their credit report through the small claims court. Unless you are an authorized agent, you will not be able to file delinquent accounts directly with the credit reporting agencies, so this is a nice benefit of the court system.

Another effective tactic is to file a lien on the property of a non-paying client. Although the process differs by state, most contractors are allowed to place a lien on any property where work has been performed within a specified time frame. Basically, when a homeowner goes to sell or refinance their house, the title company will conduct a search to clear the property's title. If any liens exist, they must be paid before the transaction can go through to closing. While you won't be able to collect until the property is sold or refinanced, at least your lien will be collecting interest while you wait.

4.3 Working with Support Staff

You may be working on your own when you first start your business, but at some point you could decide to hire people to work with you. For example, you might hire an assistant or someone to help market your company. You might hire these people as employees, or you might sign them on as contractors.

4.3.1 Employees versus Contractors

Legally, if you hire an employee, you will have to pay payroll taxes on that employee, and probably make unemployment and workers' compensation contributions to the appropriate government agency. On the other hand, you can train those employees the way you like, and you can require them to do their work at certain hours and at places you choose.

If you hire contractors, those people will have learned their job skills elsewhere. They can choose how and when to do the work. You mutually agree on what product will be delivered or what services will be performed, as well as where and when they will be performed. But you cannot require them to be at your office or anywhere else for a certain number of hours daily. It is often best to spell out what you expect and what the contractor is to do or deliver in an agreement.

Other differences between an employee and a contractor, which also apply to you as a consultant, are:

- Employees work only for you. Contractors may have other clients as well as you, and can work for any and all of them.
- Employees are paid on a regular basis. Contractors are paid per project.
- Employees work for a certain number of hours. Contractors set their own hours, as long as they get the job done. That can be great for them if they are really fast, or not so great for them if they are really slow. As long as the project is finished on time to specs, it's great for you. (On the other hand, if an employee is slow, you may end up paying more salary to get the job done in overtime, or even hiring temporary help to get things finished.)
- Employees can be fired or quit. Contractors can't be fired in the usual way while they are working under contract. You may decide to have them stop working on a project, but you will be obliged to pay them according to your contractual agreement unless you are able to renegotiate the contract or successfully sue them if you are unhappy with their work. (Of course that would only be in extreme cases; it is best to avoid lawsuits altogether!)

Even though you are not writing paychecks to contractors, but rather checks for contracting fees, there are still tax considerations. For more information about employment taxes, contact the IRS or Canada Revenue Agency.

For More Information

Before you hire, check with your local department of labor to find out all the rules and regulations required as an employer. There may be other state and federal rules and regulations that may apply to you, including: health and safety regulations, Workers' Compensation, minimum wage and unemployment insurance. Before you hire someone as an employee, it's a good idea to get some additional information concerning regulations, taxes and so forth.

In addition to your local department of labor, visit the sites below for more information:

- *Canada Business Service Centres*
  (Click on "Hiring and Managing Staff")
  www.canadabusiness.ca/gol/cbec/site.nsf/en/index.html

- *U.S. Internal Revenue Service*
  (Search for "employees and contractors")
  www.irs.gov

- *U.S. Department of Labor*
  www.dol.gov/opa/aboutdol/lawsprog.htm

4.3.2 Finding Support Staff

So, how do you find staff when you need help? There are several routes you can take, including running an ad in the classified section of your area newspaper, working with an employment service, or seeking help on an online job site such as Monster.com.

However, the first place to start is by using word of mouth to get the word out that you are looking to hire someone. Ask friends, family, and acquaintances if they know anyone who might be a good candidate to work with your business. You can also spread the word through organizations that you belong to. You can find out more about networking in section 5.3.3.

If you need help for just a limited time, you might consider contacting a temporary employee service. These services provide employees on a temporary basis. You pay the service, and the service pays the employee. It also provides benefits to the employee and takes care of payroll, taxes and so forth. You'll likely need to pay more to the service than you'd pay to a permanent employee, but if you only need help for a limited amount of time, it may be worth it.

The selection process starts with the prospective employee filling out an application. Here are some other things to look out for when prospective employees come in to fill out an application or drop off a resume:

- Are they dressed nicely? Well-groomed?
- Are they polite or do they say, "Gimme an application"?
- Are they alone? Chances are that if the potential employee can't come to fill out an application without their best friend, they can't work without their friends either.
- What does your gut instinct tell you?

4.3.3 The Interview Process

The purpose of an interview is to get to know potential applicants as much as you can in a short period of time. It is therefore important that most of that time be spent getting the applicants to talk about themselves. Most employers with limited interviewing experience spend too much time talking about the job or their business. And while that is certainly important, it won't help you figure out to whom you are talking and if that person is a good match for your store. A good rule of thumb to follow is that the applicant should do 80% of the talking.

To make the best use of your time, have a list of questions prepared in advance. This will keep the process consistent between applicants. You can always add questions that pop up based on their answers as you go along. For best results, ask the right type of questions.

To get a sense of how an employee will actually behave on the job, it is a good idea to ask "behavioral questions." Behavioral questions ask applicants to give answers based on their past behavior. An example is "Tell me about a time you had to deal with a difficult customer. What was the situation and how did you handle it?" Instead of giving hypothetical answers of what someone would do in a particular situation, the applicant must give examples of what they actually have done. While people's behavior can change, past performance is a better indicator of someone's future behavior than hypothetical answers.

You can also ask questions that communicate your company policies to discover if the applicant will have any issues in these areas. Some examples are:

- When you are working, I expect your full attention to be on my customers. I do not allow private phone calls unless it is an emergency. Is that a problem?
- It is important that we open on time. I expect my workers to be punctual. Is there anything that could keep you from being on time for every shift?

By being clear on specifics and details in the interview, you can hash out any potential problems right then and there or agree to go your own ways because it is not going to work.

What You Can and Can't Ask

You should be aware that there are some things you simply cannot ask about during a job interview. Some are illegal and others are insulting and open the door to charges of discrimination. They include questions about:

- Age
- Race
- Religion
- Marital status
- Family status or pregnancy
- Disability
- Workers Compensation claims
- Injury

- Medical condition
- Sexual orientation

4.3.4 References

Once you have found an applicant who appears to be a good fit, you can learn more by checking their references. The best references are former employers. (Former co-workers may be friends who will give glowing references no matter how well the employee performed.)

Many companies will not give you detailed information about a past employee. They are only required to give you employment dates and sometimes they will confirm salary. But many times you will be able to learn a lot about a potential applicant from a reference phone call. A good employee is often remembered fondly and even asked about by a former employer. An employer may not be able to tell you much about a bad employee for liability reasons, but they can answer the question "Is this employee eligible to be rehired?"

Here are some other additional questions from Tom Hennessy, author of the *FabJob Guide to Become a Coffee House Owner*:

- How long did this person work for you (this establishes the accuracy of their applications)?
- How well did they get along with everyone (looking for team skills)?
- Did they take direction well (code words for "did they do their job")?
- Could they work independently (or did they sit around waiting to be told what to do next)?
- How did they handle stressful situations (this is important, especially if you are busy)?

If the references make you feel comfortable, call the employee to let them know they have a job and to come in and fill out the paperwork.

5. Getting Clients

What would a business be without customers? Well, not much of anything! If your best friend and your mother are the only people who know you are a home stager, your phone won't be ringing a lot. Acquiring a steady flow of new clients is perhaps the single most important aspect of your business. You will find these invaluable clients by effectively marketing your services.

It's easy to spend so much time managing your business that you forget how essential it is to continually promote your services. In order to be successful, is it imperative to understand the significance and power of marketing.

Susan Fruit, owner of Susan Fruit Interiors, is an interior designer with over 30 years of industry experience. She is also featured in *Conversations on Success*, a book which highlights thriving professionals and their advice for reaching your goals. Susan feels that marketing is typically seen as being a good salesperson, when sales are actually just one part of the marketing process.

She offers some creative imagery to explain her concept of marketing:

> "If the circus is coming to town and you hang a sign saying, 'The circus is coming to the Fairgrounds this Saturday,' that's advertising. If you put a sign on the back of an elephant and walk him through town, that's promotion. If the elephant convinces people in town to attend the circus, then that's sales. If the elephant walks through the mayor's flowerbed, that's publicity. If you can get the mayor to laugh and talk about it, that's public relations. And, if you planned and organized the whole thing, that's marketing!"

This is an excellent analogy because high-quality marketing will require the same energy, passion, and commitment as walking an elephant through town. Simply handing out your business cards will not deliver the income you need to flourish. As the above anecdote points out, marketing your services will consist of advertising, promotions, personal selling, and public relations.

When these elements are working together, your business will grow in response. Susan adds that, "Marketing is an umbrella encompassing numerous components for the purpose of enticing people to purchase your products or services. You'll want to incorporate all of its components into your marketing plan."

This chapter will provide you with very useful insights and insider advice from professional stagers. You will learn marketing techniques which have already been tested, so that you won't have to reinvent the wheel.

5.1 Planning Your Marketing Campaign

5.1.1 Choose Your Target Markets

A good marketing plan should detail how your business is positioned in the competitive marketplace and help you define your target audience. It's wise to review the plan each year and see if you are on track to meet your stated goals.

Start with a market analysis, or SWOT, to determine your strengths, weaknesses, opportunities, and threats. Evaluating your company's internal strengths and weaknesses will give you a realistic picture of your capabilities and point out any areas that may need improvement. Looking at your opportunities and threats will prepare you to deal with your competition and other external factors. This process will also help you identify your target market.

While you are thinking about your target market, take into consideration how you approach home staging. Contributing writer Nancy Cook-Geoghegan of One Day Décor advises that "for staging, your audience is going to be the real estate agent, broker, or the homeowner who is selling without the services of a real estate agent." Nancy believes the best way to start is by summarizing what you want to accomplish with your business. She suggests that you "write a summary of what your business means to you and what services you will offer. What are your strengths, your philosophy, and who will your clients be?"

Your target market is the individual you want as your customer and who will benefit from your service offerings. Sandy Dixon, owner of Interior Arrangements Inc., likes to call these your "choice clients." Your choice clients are real estate agents. The best agents to approach are those in the winner's club or million dollar club. These successful realtors will be well established in your local area, so their experience and reputation will work to your benefit. Your secondary target market is the homeowner who is readying their home for sale. Other potential target markets include offices and retail stores which may need redesign, organizational, or merchandising services.

The fastest way to find realtors in your area is by an online search. You can search for realtors at the MLS website at **www.realtor.com** or, in Canada, **www.realtor.ca**. The home pages on both websites include a search form in which you can type your city and choose your state or province to find a list of realtors and real estate brokerages.

The Yellow Pages also lists realtors. You can also look for local or regional real estate magazines that feature homes in the area, which are usually available for free at places like grocery stores and bank lobbies.

5.1.2 Your Marketing Budget

The funds that you set aside each month to advertise your business will create your marketing budget. In order to reach your target audience, you will likely use a combination of paid and free marketing tactics. The amount of money available for use will decide the mix of methods used, so you should calculate what you can afford.

After researching how to reach your choice clients, you should evaluate which advertising mediums fit into your budget. To really start out with a bang, you can easily spend anywhere from $500 to $2000 per month in advertising costs. Of course, many new businesses are starting on a shoestring budget, so low-cost marketing tactics like networking and publicity can be relied upon until more revenue is available.

It's a good idea to start with a Yellow Pages ad, a website, and local newspaper or magazine advertising. Many small business owners find that a targeted direct mail campaign can yield nice results, and the postcards can be sent out in small batches.

After you have built up your client base, you will be able to consider what percentage of profits you can allocate towards your monthly marketing budget. A good rule of thumb is to invest about 10% to 20% of profits back into advertising.

Your start-up marketing expenses can easily cost about $500 to $1,000 for brochures, business cards, gift certificates, stationary, web page design, and web hosting. Keep in mind, there are many tools available to greatly reduce these costs. It's feasible to print your own business cards and brochures for the cost of paper and ink. Also, many web hosting companies offer affordable monthly packages along with templates for building your own website.

Examples of average monthly advertising expenses:

- Advertising in a small local newspaper or magazine, $350 to $600 per month
- Yellow Pages ad, $45 to $250 per month
- Website hosting, $9 to $55 per month

- Car signs and yard signs, one-time expense of $100 to $250
- Networking fees and association fees, $250 per year

5.1.3 Your Marketing Message

Once you know what your business philosophy will be, you can put together a consistent marketing message that expresses this to your target audience. The message should be catchy and easily remembered, and it generally becomes your company's slogan. You should also design your logo to complement your marketing message and the services you provide. Choose color schemes and font typefaces that are easy to read.

You can use the word "staging" in your marketing message. If you want to do redesign as well as staging, you should use a more open message, such as "Remix, Renew, and Stage Your Home." You should be consistent when it comes to your slogan and logo, so use them on your business cards, website, brochures, and any other correspondence.

Here are some sample marketing messages from other stagers and redesigners:

- Nancy Cook-Geoghegan of One Day Décor:
  "Creating Picture Perfect Homes."
- Debra Gould, creator of the The Staging Diva® program:
  "Sell High. Sell Fast. Sell Smart."
- Sandy Dixon of Interior Arrangements, Inc.:
  "A Training, Speaking & Coaching Company Specializing in Interior & Real Estate Staging."
- Moona Masri-Whitice of Perfectlyou Décor:
  "Remix Re-Organize Redesign What You Own."

5.2 Marketing Tools

5.2.1 Printed Materials

Your printed materials include business cards, stationery (such as letterhead, envelopes, and mailing labels), and other marketing materials such as brochures.

If you have a computer with a high quality laser or ink jet printer, you may be able to inexpensively print professional looking materials from your own computer. Free templates for the print materials you are likely to need in your business can be found online.

HP offers templates for a variety of programs at **www.hp.com/sbso/productivity/office**. For example, you can create a matching set of stationery (business cards, letterhead, envelopes) in Microsoft Word or a presentation in PowerPoint. The site includes free online classes and how-to guides to help you design your own marketing materials. Another excellent resource is the Microsoft Office Online Templates Homepage at **http://office.microsoft.com/en-us/templates/**. At this site you can search a database to find templates for:

- Business stationery (envelopes, faxes, labels, letters, memos, etc.)
- Marketing materials (brochures, flyers, newsletters, postcards, etc.)
- Other business documents (expense reports, invoices, receipts, time sheets, etc.)

As an alternative to printing materials yourself, and for materials that won't fit through your printer (such as folders), consider using a company that provides printing services. Beautiful stationery can convey to prospective clients that you have a good eye and a high standard of excellence. Your printed materials can be easily designed, paid for and delivered without leaving the house. Here are links to some companies that provide printing services for small businesses:

- *FedEx Office*
  www.fedex.com/us/office/copyprint/online/
- *Acecomp Plus – Printing Solutions*
  www.acecomp.com/printing.asp
- *The Paper Mill Store*
  www.thepapermillstore.com
- *VistaPrint*
  www.vistaprint.com

While the resources listed above can help with all your printing needs, here is some advice about two types of materials that are particularly important for marketing purposes – business cards and brochures.

Business Cards

The first thing on your list of marketing tools is your business cards. This is one item that you can't do without as a home stager. A business card gives clients the essential contact information for your business, and every time you hand one out you should think of it as a mini advertisement.

The basic information to list on your business cards includes:

- Your name
- Your title (such as President or Owner)
- Your company name
- Your contact information (phone numbers, email address, fax number)
- Your web address

In addition, consider including the following items to promote you and your consulting services.

- Professional memberships and certifications (e.g. Member, International Association of Home Staging Professionals)
- Your specializations and services offered
- Company logo
- Your mailing address

Keep business cards the standard size, 2 x 3 ½ inches, and if possible, invest in a sturdy card that has a good weight and feel to it. The cost of business cards can vary depending on how much or how little of the work you do creating them. You can make your own business cards inexpensively if you own or have access to a computer. Office supply stores sell sheets of cards that can go through any type of printer.

Sample Business Cards

Card #1: Front

Remix Re-Organize Redesign what you have

Moona Masri-Whitice, I.R.I.S.
Interior Decorator and Redesign Specialist

954-650-1470
mmw@perfectlyoudecor.net
www.perfectlyoudecor.net

Card #1: Back

Specializing in creating spaces that redesign lives!

Color Consultation and Feng - Shui
Same Day Decorating - Redecoramos su casa en un dia
Home and Office Organization
Home Staging
Move Ins
Creamos espacios que definen tu personalidad y gusto!

www.perfectlyoudecor.net

Card #2: Front

THE NEXT STAGE The Redesign Specialist

HOME STAGING SERVICES BY
Ima Stager
IRIS Certified: Member ASID, CID, IADA

123 Main Street,
Anytown, USA

Tel: (123) 345-6789 Fax: (123) 345-6790
designer@thenextstage.com
www.thenextstage.com

Card #2: Back

Residential and Commercial Services

Room by Room Consultations and Makeovers
Realty Staging and Advice
Equity Enhancement—Sell Your Home for More Money
Creating Curb Appeal
Interior Decorating
Interior Redesign
Feng Shui
Home and Office Organizing
Color Consultations
Clutter Management
Landscaping Service
Residential Remodeling
Shopping Service

You can also hire a graphic artist to design a logo, do the layout and even arrange for printing. Most print shops have a design specialist on staff to help with these matters as well. Whichever way you decide to go, make sure your business card is a reflection of you and your home staging business.

When ordering your cards from a printer, the more you order the less expensive they are. When you order 500 cards, for example, the cost is minimal, starting around $50 depending on how many colors you have on your card and the card stock you use. Shop around to see where you can get the best deal.

Another alternative when you're just starting out is to use free business cards from VistaPrint.com. You can order 250 cards from them, using a variety of contemporary designs, and you only pay for shipping. The only catch is that they print their company logo on the back. If you don't mind having their logo on the back of your business cards, this is very economical. If you prefer not to have another company's name printed on the back of your business cards you can order 250 cards for about $20 plus shipping from VistaPrint without their logo.

Once your cards are printed, always keep some on hand, as you never know who you might run into. Keeping your business cards in a case is more professional than keeping them scattered across the bottom of your briefcase or bag. It will also ensure that you only hand out pristine cards, and not a worn or stained card.

Brochures

You will have many opportunities to give out your business card. But there are also times to give out brochures; for example, when you give a presentation at a networking meeting (see section 5.3) or when people seem particularly interested in your services. You should also provide some to the companies with whom you do a lot of business in case someone asks them if they know a home stager they could recommend.

Brochures give prospective clients an overview of what your business is about. Some home stagers choose to develop very detailed brochures while others prefer a clean look with less detail. If you decide to create a brochure for your business, it should of course contain your company name and contact information, including your web address. It can also include information such as:

- Information about the services you provide
- A description of your professional qualifications
- Before and after photographs of home staging projects you have completed
- A photograph of you
- Testimonial quotes from satisfied clients

Also, be sure to use benefit-rich statements in your brochure, such as:

- Staging Helps Real Estate Agents Get More Listings
- Staging Helps Real Estate Agents/Homeowners Sell Their Homes Faster
- Staging Helps Real Estate Agents/Homeowners Sell for Top Dollar

You can purchase low-cost stock photos (a few dollars each) through websites such as **www.istockphoto.com** or **www.dreamstime.com**. If you want to publish photos of your own clients, whether on your website or in print, be sure you have them sign a release form that gives you permission to use the images in any of your promotional materials without compensation. Most people are happy to have their images used in such a positive way but there may be exceptions. On the next page is a sample of a release form you can use.

If you are printing only a few copies of your brochure, you may be able to find nice paper at your local office supply store or one of the websites listed earlier in this section, which you can run through your printer. You can use software such as Microsoft Publisher to design and print your own brochures. SmartDraw also offers free trial software that you can download and use to design your brochures at home. Visit **www.smartdraw.com/specials/business-flyers.asp**.

For a professional look you can use a service such as VistaPrint (**www.vistaprint.com**) or a printer in your area to do it for you. Look online or in the Yellow Pages under "Printers." The cost starts at around $50 at VistaPrint, and can go much higher for other printing companies printing with color and glossy paper.

Many printers will have an in-house design department who can do the artwork for you, but make sure you have a hand in developing the text. You are the best-qualified person to describe what your business is all about. Also, check for any typos in your phone number, email address or other contact information or you will be paying the printer to fix 1,000 brochures or doing it by hand.

Sample Release Form

I hereby give (insert your name) permission to use my photograph taken of me on (insert date) at (insert location) for promotional, on-line or commercial purposes. I am of legal age.

____________________ ____________________

(Print Name) *(Date)*

____

(Signature)

5.2.2 Your Portfolio

An essential tool to have in your marketing arsenal is your portfolio. This visual presentation is an ideal way to introduce your clients to all the services you provide and show them pictures of your work. This also provides an opportunity to explain the process of home staging along with key benefits and industry statistics. Sandy Dixon feels that all stagers should build a portfolio because "it's an ice breaker for initial meetings, and it validates you as an expert." Think of a portfolio as a window into your business.

While not mandatory, you might consider obtaining written photo releases from your clients, so they are aware that photos of their homes could be used in your portfolio or advertising. At a minimum, get their verbal approval to use the photos.

A standard portfolio usually consists of the following elements:

- A one-page bio with your photograph attached. This should touch on your professional life as a stager by listing your training, education, experience, and your marketing message.
- Before and after photographs with descriptive captions. Include about six to twelve sets of photos representing your own work.
- Industry statistics and selling points that will educate your clients about the benefits of your services.
- Certificates of membership in affiliated industry organizations.
- Training certificates and awards.
- Media coverage that you have received or articles you have written.
- Client testimonials which praise your work.
- A professional-looking binder or presentation book with sheet protectors to hold the above mentioned items.

A portfolio offers a prospective customer proof that you have the skills and creativity to do the job. Read on to find out how to get items for your portfolio and how to put it together. At the end of this section you'll find some tips on how to create a portfolio if you don't yet have materials from actual events.

Photographs

They say a picture speaks a thousand words, and nowhere is this more true than when you are trying to sell yourself as being creative, imaginative and organized.

Try to arrange to get photographs from every home you work on. In fact, with the first few staging projects you plan for friends or relatives, you might offer your home staging services for free in exchange for photographs to put into your portfolio. While you won't include every photograph in your portfolio, it is a good idea to have as many photos as possible to choose from.

When selecting photographs, remember that your portfolio should be a collection of your best examples, ideally showing before and after images. Most clients do not have time to look through hundreds of photographs, so be selective about what to include.

One suggested guideline is to choose 15-20 photographs of work you are really proud of (if you have that many different photos). It's ideal if you have staged several different types of homes, so you can show some variety. If not, simply use what you have.

Letters of Recommendation

The best letters of recommendation are those written by clients whose homes you have staged. However, you can also include letters of recommendation from past employers if the letters say good things about your abilities in areas that are important in the home staging business, such as interpersonal skills and organizational ability. You can also include appropriate thank-you notes you have received.

Every time you stage a home for someone — even a friend or family member (preferably with a different last name from yours!) — ask for a letter of recommendation. When you ask for a letter, keep in mind that many people are busy, so they are more likely to do what you ask if you can make it as easy as possible.

To help get the kind of recommendation letter you want, and make the job easier on the person writing the letter, you could supply a list of points they might mention. For example, you could mention:

- what you did (write it out for them — chances are you remember exactly what you did more clearly than they might)
- how you got along well with everyone you worked with
- how you came up with many creative ideas
- how you handled every detail so well they didn't have to worry about a thing
- that everyone has commented on how beautiful the staged home was

Of course, all these things don't have to be included in a single letter! The specifics will depend on the particular job you did, but even a few glowing sentences can help you look good to clients.

If you feel your relative or friend will not write a great letter – even if you specifically suggest of what to include – you can offer to compose the letter yourself and have them simply supply the signature. You should have a couple of different letters written specifically for this purpose and propose one of them as an alternative.

Here is a sample reference letter:

Sample Recommendation Letter

Dear Lola Stager,

Joe and I would like to take this opportunity to thank you again for the wonderful job you did staging our home. We never realized our house could be so organized and well decorated!

Your ideas and creative little touches were so unexpected and yet so perfect.

You promised our house would sell faster and that is exactly what you delivered. What you didn't tell us was what a pleasure it would be to work with you. Your professionalism and organizational skill in dealing with the contractors we hired to finish up all the minor repairs that were necessary impressed us very much. We could not have finished everything up so quickly if we had tried to do it ourselves.

We will certainly recommend your service to family and friends and wish you success in the years to come.

Sincerely,
Joanne Smith

P.S. I thought you might like to know that we had three competing bids on our house and sold it for $12,000 more than our original asking price!

TIP: A recommendation letter should preferably not mention that you worked for free. You want to give the impression that your work has value, and a customer may assume the reason you received such a glowing recommendation is because you didn't charge anything. Remember, good work is good work no matter how much you were paid for it.

What Else to Include

Your portfolio can include anything else that could impress someone who is considering hiring you. For example, if you have a certificate of membership in a home staging or interior decorating association or for completion of a home staging course, put the actual certificate in your portfolio. If that's not possible, include a photocopy or a photograph of the certificate.

Likewise, if your home staging business has been mentioned in a newspaper or magazine story, you could include a clipping or photocopy of the published article. Later in this chapter, you will find information about how to write articles for publication, and other ways to establish your reputation as an event planning expert.

Putting It All Together

There are several different options for displaying the materials in your portfolio. One possibility is to put everything into a professional-looking three-ring binder with plastic sheet covers to protect the pages. If you wish, you can mount your photographs and other portfolio materials onto thin cardboard. All of these supplies are available from any office supply store.

Another possibility is to use a portfolio case, which you can buy at an art supply store (check the Yellow Pages). Portfolio or presentation cases comes in a variety of sizes (e.g. 11″ x 14″, 14″ x 17″, 17″ x 22″) and cost from about $15 to $150-plus, depending on the size, material, and how fancy you want it to be. However, clients are interested in what is inside the case, so you don't need to spend a lot of money on the case itself (e.g. you could get vinyl instead of leather). The following websites have some examples: **www.dickblick.com** (do a search for portfolio) and **www.keysan.com//ksu0601.htm**.

Another option is to have a series of folders marked with the date type of staged property you did, and who you did the staging for. Include these folders in a master folder (or portfolio case) so you can keep all your details together.

How to Create a Portfolio without Experience

If you don't yet have materials from actual homes you have staged, you can create materials. For example, you could come up with an idea for staging your own home, then produce a collage of what you would do for that. Include a floor plan and layout, create a room-by-room checklist of issues/problems/suggestions for staging each room, etc.

If you have a camera and can take decent photos, take some "before" photos, then take some "after" photos when you are finished. As soon as you've staged a home or two, you will have pictures from an actual project and can drop the others from your portfolio.

You can use any of the methods described above to display your materials. However, it can be particularly impressive to put your samples onto picture matting or heavy poster board, which you can buy from an art supply store. (Check the Yellow Pages.) Your board can be white, black, or another color that you feel looks best with your samples. The size can be 14" x 17", 15" x 20", or any size that allows you to effectively display the materials.

You can arrange the samples on a board in a way that looks most attractive to you. While you can use glue to attach your samples, using double-sided tape can help you avoid any bumps caused by glue.

5.2.3 Your Website

Customers will expect to find you on the Internet. A substantial number of people now use online Yellow Pages and search engines to find businesses. In addition, the tendency towards using this resource is rapidly growing in popularity.

Nancy Cook-Geoghegan of One Day Décor believes that "a website is a must, and if you don't have one in today's market, you will be left behind. However, it shouldn't serve as a substitute for all the other marketing tools. It's just a way to keep your business available 24/7. For even better performance, link your website to as many strategic allies as possible."

Nancy shares the following tips on the topic of websites:

- To collect ideas of style and formatting visit well-designed sites from known stagers and redesign specialists. Do so by searching for 'home staging' or 'home redesign' through a search engine like Google, or you can log on to an association such as **www.stagedhomes.com** or **www.weredesign.com** to look at other established business websites.

- Optimize your website by using key words for search engines to pick up, such as: interior decorating, interior design, furniture arrangement, room arranging, furniture, home furnishings, home decorator, use what you have, redecorate, room makeovers, home improvements, move-ins, home staging, real estate staging, prepare a home for sale, open house, furniture placement, arranging a room.

- Include a separate web page for each main topic: services, information about you, before and after gallery, tips, and products that you will sell.

Your website can be an important tool for marketing your services. It gives prospective clients an opportunity to learn more about you and your services at their convenience any time of day. It may also introduce you to new clients you might otherwise not encounter through other marketing activities.

What to Include on Your Website

Any information you would include in a brochure (described in section 5.2.1) can also be included on your website. Here are some ideas of what to include on your website to get you started:

- Home page with links to navigate through your site.

- "About Us" page so that your customers can learn more about you and your company. This should include your credentials and a photograph of you.
- A way to contact you, including at least your company name, telephone number and email address. This should ideally be on every page, but you can also have a "Contact Us" page with your business mailing address, fax number and other contact information.
- Information about your services and the benefits you offer to potential clients.
- Testimonial quotes from satisfied clients.
- Helpful information you have written such as business articles, checklists, advice, and other content that shows your expertise. Adding new content on a regular basis can keep people returning to your site.
- To build up a contact list, you could offer a free email newsletter, and include a place at your website where visitors can subscribe. Your newsletter could include articles about the types of services you offer and information about holiday specials, events, and other news. Your newsletters can also be posted online.

TIP: You can send out email newsletters inexpensively through a company such as Constant Contact at **www.constantcontact.com**. The cost starts at $15 per month for a list of up to 500 people, and a free trial is available.

Getting Online

Designing Your Website

Clients will judge the quality of your business and services by what they see on your site. If you don't have the time or expertise to design a polished website yourself, you can have a professional web developer build and maintain your site. There is no shortage of web designers, so consult your local phone directory or search online for one in your area. You can also try interior decorating business templates, such as **www.creatingonline.com/webmaster/templates/homeinterior.htm.**

If you are already experienced at creating web pages, or learn quickly, you can design your website yourself using a program such as Adobe Dreamweaver or a free program like SeaMonkey (available at **www.seamonkey-project.org**). You may also use the website development tools offered by domain and hosting companies, described below.

Getting a Domain Name

To present a professional image and make your web address easier for clients to remember, consider getting your own domain name, such as www.yourstorename.com. There are a number of sites where you can search for and register a domain name. One web host we have found that provides good service for a low cost is **www.godaddy.com**. Microsoft also offers a quick search for domain name availability using their sign-up feature at **http://smallbusiness.officelive.com**. (They'll also help you to set up a free website for your business.)

If your preferred domain name is available, but you're not yet ready with your website, you can also "park" your domain. This means that you register the domain so that someone else does not take it before you're up and running with your business website. You then park the domain with your web host.

Finding a Host

Once you register your domain, you will need to find a place to "host" it. You can host it with the same company where you've registered the name. For example, if you register a domain name through GoDaddy, you might use their hosting services to put your website online.

You may also be able to put up free web pages through your Internet Service Provider (the company that gives you access to the Internet). However, if you want to use your own domain name, you'll likely need to pay for hosting. Yahoo! also offers a popular low-cost web hosting service at **http://smallbusiness.yahoo.com/webhosting/**. You can find a wide variety of other companies that provide hosting services by doing an online search. Before choosing a web host, read the article about web hosting scams at **www.webhostingchoice.com/scams.shtml** to help you avoid hosting problems.

Promoting Your Site

No matter how much you spend on creating your website, if people don't know it exists, it won't help your business. Make certain you list your site on all your business forms, cards, and brochures. Encourage people to visit your site by mentioning it as often as you can, for example, whenever you write an article, give a presentation, or are interviewed by the media.

Make sure people can find your website by getting it into the search engines and listing it with industry websites. While some sites and search engines charge a fee to guarantee that your website will be included in their directory, you can submit your website for free to Google at **www.google.com/submityourcontent/index.html**. Once you're on Google, your site is likely to be found by other search engines as well.

Your web hosting company may offer a search engine submission service for an additional fee. You can find information about "optimizing" your website, to help it rank higher on search engines, at the Search Engine Watch website at **http://searchenginewatch.com** and at Google's Webmaster Help Center at **www.google.com/support/webmasters**.

In addition to the free search engine listings, you can advertise on the search engines. See section 5.3.1 for more information.

5.2.4 Your Elevator Pitch

Imagine you have stepped onto an elevator with someone who has just asked what you do. During that elevator ride, you'll have about 60 seconds to give a brief explanation of your business and services. Because this person – like most other people you meet – may be someone else who could become a client or otherwise help your business, you want to say something to get the listener immediately interested in you and your business.

What you would say in this situation is your "elevator pitch." And while most occasions to tell people about your business won't happen while you're riding an elevator, a well-crafted elevator pitch may be the single most effective, and least expensive business development tool you can have. Your elevator pitch, like your business card, is a basic business marketing tool. But it can be particularly powerful in helping you generate sales. Here is advice on creating an elevator pitch adapted from Marg Archibald, co-author of the *FabJob Guide to Become a Business Consultant*:

Whether you are speaking to a group or to a single person, the principles of a good pitch are the same. It needs to be simple and memorable, and because we store memories based on the emotions attached to them, a pitch that generates feelings is going to be remembered. In home staging, saying something memorable that offers proof you can help them sell their house faster and for more money is the strongest card you can play.

An effective elevator pitch provides people with memorable words they can tell others and creates positive impressions that could lead to more word-of-mouth business for you. Your elevator pitch is always targeted, as closely as possible, to your audience. When you're pitching to a group you focus on what is common to the group. Your elevator pitch is a chance to make the group sit up and pay attention because you connect with what matters to them.

When you are speaking to one individual, two things change. You can tailor your pitch very specifically to that person, plus you can turn the speech into a dialogue in less than one minute since you already have the person's attention. Note that the core elevator pitch is the same, but how you fit it into a conversation changes.

Group Elevator Pitch

You have 60 seconds to connect with the group and their priorities. You open with your name, title and company name. You briefly describe your business and an overview of your services. The key here is to be brief. You sketch out the things you do that would most interest this particular group. You outline the kinds of clients you serve (ideally clients just like them), and tell a story proving how effective you are. This may include a quote from a happy client. You express interest in working for them or receiving referrals. You close with a memorable phrase, repeating your name and company. This is perfect when it is your turn to stand up at a luncheon and introduce yourself, although it is a bit too long in one-on-one situation.

One-On-One Elevator Pitch

People can tune you out in 10 seconds or less. An engaging, interactive, one-on-one elevator pitch gets the same information across that you would present to a group but involves the listener in dialogue sooner.

First, you need to find out more about the person you're speaking with. Use every bit of information you can glean about the person you're speaking to in order to make your pitch relevant. Your observations are providing you information from the time you approach each other. Keep the focus on the other person.

- Where might you have met before?
- Is he or she wearing a name tag? Does it list his or her company? Is that company one you could work with?
- What is his or her title?
- Who has he or she just been talking to? Have you picked up any additional information from that observation?
- How does the other person react to your name tag?
- How confident does he or she appear to be in this group?

When you initiate the conversation, you can open with: "Hello. I'm *(your first and last name)* with *(your company name)*. I don't think we've met." Then pause to get the other person's name and if possible any other info on what he or she does. When the other person asks what you do, you can follow simple steps:

Step 1 - Connection

- "I work with people like you."
- "I work with businesses like yours."
- "I work in your industry."

If you know absolutely nothing about the other person, you can say, "I work with *(types of people/businesses)*."

Step 2 - Promise

"I increase home values by improving the look of home interiors." *(i.e. whatever you do, very simply)*

Step 3 - Proof

"Clients say/my last client said/most people who use my services say…"

Step 4 - Probe

Connect the proof back to the other person and whether they have used a home stager, or any difficulties the other person has in selling homes: "Do you find that some homes in particular are difficult to sell?/Do you have that problem?/How do you handle that problem?"

Step 5 - Close

If this is a strong prospect, you probe further and gently work toward trying to set up a meeting. (See the sample below for an example of how to do this.)

If this is a weak prospect, you can ask if he or she knows of anyone that might be interested in your services. Consider that every single person you meet is a conduit to people that will be helpful even if they are not actual prospects.

Sample One-on-One Elevator Pitch

Connection

"I work with realtors in the same real estate market as you."

Promise

"I help clients sell their homes faster and for more money."

Proof

"I just finished a home staging project that helped my client sell their home in less than one week, and they received $10,000 more than their asking price."

Probe

"Have you ever used a home stager for the homes you sell? Would you consider trying a home staging service?"

Close

(Strong Prospect) "I'm interested in chatting with you further. I may be able to help out there and make some improvements to that house you're having difficulty selling. I have an opening on Tuesday afternoon next week if you'd like to discuss this further."

(Weak Prospect) "I'm interesting in creating value for realtors and homeowners." Insert some chatting about the real estate market and its problems, relate to his or her issues as a realtor. Feel your way to gradually asking: "Do you know anyone having trouble selling homes? Could you suggest anyone in this room you think I should meet?"

Practice Your Pitch

Armed with an elevator pitch that you have practiced until it sounds and feels natural, you can practice on friends, family, colleagues and acquaintances. Ask for honest feedback. Pay attention to their suggestions and make any changes necessary to create a more effective pitch. Once you are comfortable with your elevator pitch, you'll be able to use it to market your business.

Other Marketing Tools

People love anything that is free. If you put your company's logo, phone number, and website on promotional items, you have something to give away that will market your business.

Think about ordering inexpensive items like pens, pencils, notepads, magnets, key chains, coffee mugs, and mini tape measures. Start out small, so that you don't put a strain on your marketing budget. As time progresses, you can move on to larger items like t-shirts, hats, tote bags, and mouse pads. Give away these promotional items at home shows, industry trade shows, seminars, and client consultations. Use them as a thank you gift for the referral of a new customer.

Another low-cost, highly visible method of advertising is the yard sign. These little billboards are commonly referred to as real estate signs. Many successful home stagers place signs in their client's yard while working in a house, because it draws the attention of the neighbors. Make sure the community where you are working allows yard signs before using them.

Order a supply of small, portable easel signs which you can display at retail stores, home shows, or seminars. Create an 8″ x 10″ sign that includes photos of your work and your business contact information. Have several signs laminated and use them with easels. A sign shop can also mount the sign on foam and add a folding easel to the back.

Distribute flyers or laminated tip sheets at consultations, real estate offices, trade shows, and association events. For a unique approach, format the tip sheet as a bookmark or calendar, so that it is memorable and useful. Possible topics for a flyer or tip sheet include changing the focal point of a room, adding color to your walls, creating a romantic bedroom, and the benefits of staging homes for sale.

Some good vendors for items like this include **www.branders.com** and **www.4imprint.com**.

5.3 Marketing Techniques

In this section we'll look at a variety of marketing techniques, including advertising, free publicity, networking, and promotional events. Consider as many of these techniques as possible to help you get the word out about who you are and what you do. Generating clients from marketing is not formulaic and not every strategy works for every home stager with the same success. The key is to determine what combination works best for you.

5.3.1 Advertising

Along with low-cost marketing activities like public relations and networking, you will also likely have a need for paid advertising. This usually consists of paying to have your message placed in a specific media outlet to target a specific audience. Until you have a steady stream of referral business, you will need to promote your company in other ways.

Advertising allows you to control who you reach and the frequency with which you do so. Your marketing budget will determine the size of the ad you can place, the medium you can use, and how long the ad will run. Since advertising can be expensive, you should make sure the medium you select reaches your target audience and provides you with results.

Before you begin an advertising campaign, it is vital to do some research. Review the advertising mediums for which you might be interested in placing your ad, such as local magazines, newspapers, or the Internet. Pay attention to what your competition is doing to promote their business and evaluate what you will do differently to stand apart from them.

The best advertising is about answering the customer's concerns. You must show them that you have all the answers to their problems. They have a need and you exist to fulfill it. Here are some examples of possible advertising messages:

- "Does your home décor need a boost? Let us help!"
- "Selling your home? Call me to sell it faster and for top dollar!"
- "Messy home? We can organize it for you!"
- "Need some color in your life? A color consultation is just what the doctor ordered!"

Booking an Ad

Once your marketing budget is in place and the proper medium has been chosen to reach your target audience, you are ready to book an ad. The process of placing an advertising order is usually made easier with the help of a sales representative. They will provide you with rates, discounts, requirements, and recommendations for your specific business type. In most cases, one call is all it takes to get a sales rep working on your behalf, but some persistence may be required when you are seen as a small fish in the advertising pond.

In general, you will be asked to sign a contract to begin running your ad. Be sure to review the terms of the contract and get any questions answered before signing it. You will have to decide how long the ad will run, what size it will be, and what elements to include.

Keep in mind that advertising is a way to generate and maintain a presence in the marketplace, while also producing a decent response rate. Even though people may not call you immediately, it's important to be the first company that comes to mind when they need a home stager or when someone asks them about such a service.

Designing an Ad

If you are completely new to advertising, it might be helpful to enlist the services of a marketing consultant, a graphic designer, or a copywriter. In addition, the publications you advertise with will most likely have an art department to help design your ad. It pays to follow your instincts when advertising, but you should also get the opinions of professionals who create ads for a living.

The images used to convey your message and the key words chosen are very important. You should present a professional image that tells the potential customer about the benefits of using your services. Use clear, quality images that show your best work or use stock photography resources. Keep your copy brief and informative, but be sure to include your marketing message, logo, phone number, and website. Whenever it's feasible, use full-color or spot-color elements to draw attention to your ad.

Including an offer can help increase the customer response rate. Try offering a free half-hour consultation or 15% off any service. Mention your professional memberships or the fact that you are insured and bonded, if applicable. Some business owners like to insert a reassuring pledge in their advertising, such as "Your satisfaction is guaranteed."

Where to Advertise

There are countless places to advertise your services. As you have probably noticed in your own home, there are hundreds of businesses competing for your attention on a daily basis. Now, you must join this advertising race. Sift through all the local advertising you encounter at home and around town. Consider which mediums or ads held your attention and why.

For the most part, the best choices for advertising in this industry are:

- Yellow Pages (print and online)
- Newspapers (classified and display ads)
- Direct mail
- Community publications
- TV (cable companies)

Yellow Pages

The first place to begin your advertising campaign is your local Yellow Pages. These directories are a powerful tool both in print and on the Internet. If you request a business phone line, then a complimentary line listing in the Yellow Pages and white pages will be automatically included. As your budget allows, consider upgrading to a small ad or a bolded listing with your website address. If you are using your cell phone or another number for your business calls, you must solicit the directory to include your information.

The cost of an enhanced listing will depend on the features selected and how many yellow page books are involved. A large metropolitan market may require several books in order to cover all areas. In addition, some markets have multiple companies distributing books such as AT&T Yellow Pages, Yellow Book, and Verizon SuperPages. You should size-up the current directories available in your area and find out what books are the most popular with your friends and family.

Almost all phone book directories are printed once a year. Missing their deadlines will cost your business a whole year of advertising. Generally, the books are distributed in the fall and early spring, but the closing dates for the ads can be months before that.

Consider listing your business under the following categories: Real Estate Consultants, Interior Decorators, Home Décor, Interior Design Consultants, or Home Improvements. Look at who is currently listed in each relevant category, and ask your directory sales representative for their suggestions as well. If you will be working from home, you may want to omit your street address from the yellow page listing or use a P.O. Box address instead.

You should also consider a listing with online yellow page directories to increase your exposure, especially if you have a website. The companies that print the books usually have a package that includes an online listing with their Internet Yellow Pages.

Newspapers

Every city or metro area has newspapers serving the region. They are usually delivered to people's homes by subscription or bought at newsstands. Many potential customers scan their local newspaper daily for sales, deals, and coupons. Unfortunately, newspaper advertising can be pricey based on the size of your market. This is also a medium where frequency is key, so be prepared to run your ad for at least a month or longer.

If you decide to advertise in the newspaper, try placing your ad in the Real Estate, Home, or Lifestyle section. You may even find a Home & Business Services section in the classifieds that is more affordable than display advertising inside the paper. Also, your local newspaper may be delighted to have you write a weekly column on home décor or staging. In addition, you pay to have your flyers inserted into local news publications.

You should also consider community newspapers that cover specific areas in your local region. These smaller papers will often have better rates than the larger newspapers and would be a good fit for a small business.

Direct Mail

Another way to get your message in the hands of your target market is to mail them a postcard, brochure, or flyer. The response rate is typically about two percent, but it can be higher based on your market and the offer. The initial step in this process is obtaining a mailing list that meets your criteria for choice clients. Look up mailing list companies in the Yellow Pages or contact a printer who handles mailings. There are also online resources like InfoUSA (**www.infousa.com**) that allow you to download mailing lists for homeowners as well as businesses like real estate agents.

After you have a clean mailing list, you'll know the quantity of postcards or flyers needed. Analyze your marketing budget and decide how many you will mail out in the first batch. Check with the company who printed your business cards and see what their rates are for postcards. You'll get a price break for higher quantities, so print extra pieces for any planned future mailings. If you do order extras, be sure to exclude dates or information that will become outdated. An oversized full-color postcard will grab the most attention from consumers.

Door hangers are another form of direct marketing which can be very cost effective. Whether you use a flyer or an actual die-cut door hanger, this type of advertisement cuts through mailbox clutter since it's placed on the front door of each home. Once you have your door hangers printed, all that's left is to walk your target neighborhoods and tag each door. Also, most cities have local contractors or services that will distribute the door hangers for you. With some effort, door hangers can be cheaper than mailing postcards and get you a higher response rate.

Community Publications

You will find various free community magazines in your local coffee shops, bookstores, and convenience stores. These smaller distribution magazines are usually printed weekly and target local neighborhoods for a fraction of the price of other periodicals.

There are plenty of other local publications to look into as well. Try seeking out school newsletters and directories, homeowner association newsletters, religious magazines, local shopping guides, and apartment community newsletters.

If you enjoy writing, offer to write an article on staging for one of these publications. This will get your name out there and establish credibility for your business.

Television

Television is a wonderful medium for visually showing your services. While you may need to build up your marketing budget before trying it, advertising on television is surprisingly within reach for a small business.

Nancy Cook-Geoghegan of One Day Décor is proof that television advertising can be affordable when you go through a local cable company. After setting up an appointment with her local cable provider, she then worked with the sales representative to narrow her focus to the audience she wanted to reach. They decided on a plan that targeted specific areas on certain days during select programs, all for a reasonable cost of $1,400 per month. Nancy feels that "placing an ad on a cable network is much like placing an ad in the newspaper."

Here are the basic considerations to review before starting the process:

- What is your budget?
- Who is your target audience?
- Will your viewers be home during the day, evening, or weekends?
- Which programs or networks are watched by your target audience?
- Are there preferred areas that you would like to reach?
- Who will produce your commercial and how much will it cost? Will you own the commercial if the cable company produces it?

In order to optimize your cable TV advertising dollars, you must do your homework and research the programming. Your commercial should be viewed at least two to three times per day by your target audience to gain recognition and produce results.

Nancy's advice is to "develop a commercial that grabs attention and also repeats your company name both on-screen and in the voiceover." She also suggests using "still photos or arranging for a crew to film you on the job, capturing before and after shots of your project."

You can also locate residential communities with their own cable access stations used to post announcements and local services. This is an even more affordable way to use television advertising for your business.

Online Advertising

In addition to or instead of an online Yellow Pages ad, you can look into other companies that specialize in online listings. One such service is Superpages.com. They offer a free business listing service as well as an enhanced version for a fee. Check their website at **www.superpages.com** for details.

Many businesses also use "pay-per-click" advertising to attract prospective clients. This involves paying for every visitor that a search engine sends to your website. You can find information about using pay-per-click advertising on Google, including how to target Internet users in your city, at **https://adwords.google.com**. Other sites you can advertise on include Yahoo!, MSN.com, and Ask.com.

If you choose specific search terms that few other advertisers have bid on, you may be able to attract some visitors to your website for as little as five cents each. However, pay-per-click costs can add up quickly and some of the people clicking on your ads may simply be curious (for example, students doing research) and not serious prospects for your business. So you should set a maximum dollar amount per day and monitor your results to determine if this type of advertising is effective for you.

Online Directories and Affiliate Listings

In order to network with others in the industry and draw customers to your website, you should register with online directories and affiliate listings. Such websites allow you to reach clients who are specifically looking for your services, and they give customers your website address and your phone number. Since your target audience will have more opportunities to find you, these listings are a great source of client referrals.

There are basically two types of industry directories out there—those that accept listings for a fee and those that require you to be a graduate of their program. If you decide to complete a training workshop, then you should register with their affiliate listing as a starting point. There is usually an annual registration fee attached to membership in these affiliate directories.

Some directories are not membership-driven organizations or associations. They will list your business information for a fee, whether you have completed a training course or simply have experience in the industry. Two such sites are the Interior Redesign and Home Staging Directory (**www.interiorredesigndirectory.com**) and At Home on Main Street (**www.athomeonmainstreet.com/services/find_a_redesigner.cfm**).

5.3.2 Free Media Publicity

One of the best ways to market—with potentially excellent results for minimal cost—is to get free publicity in the media (magazines, newspapers, radio, television, and online). While you don't have the final say over what gets reported, the exposure can give a boost to your business. This section describes a variety of ways home stagers can get publicity.

> **TIP:** Subscribe to Help a Reporter Out at **www.helpareporter.com** to receive a free email newsletter containing requests from reporters who are seeking experts to interview.

Newspaper and Magazine Publicity

One way to get a story written about your business is to send a press release (also called a "news release") to a writer, magazine editor, or the editor of the appropriate section of the newspaper. The ideal press release is a single page and should be written so that it could be published "as is." Read the magazine or section of the paper where you would like to be published and use a similar writing style for your own news release.

In order to get published, your press release should read like a story, not an advertisement. A press release that simply announces you have started your business is not likely to get published, unless there is something unusual about your business. Instead, consider issuing press releases to announce events or community activities that your business is involved with (see section 5.3.4 for information about promotional events).

Here is a quick list of tips for writing a press release. For additional tips on writing news releases visit **www.publicityinsider.com/release.asp** and **www.xpresspress.com/PRnotes.html**.

- Make sure the press release is newsworthy. A community event is newsworthy. A new business is not, unless there is something particularly interesting about the business.
- Give your press release a strong lead paragraph that answers the six main questions: who, what, where, when, why, and how.
- Keep it short. Aim for a maximum of 500 words.
- Include contact information at the end of the press release so that reporters can get more information.

Most magazines and newspapers publish contact information for their editors. If the editor's name is not published in the paper, you can call and ask the receptionist. Newspapers may have dozens of editors, so make sure you send your submission to the appropriate one (for example, the Lifestyle Editor).

As an alternative to writing a press release, you could find out who the editor is, and either phone or send a brief "pitch letter" by email, fax or mail to suggest an idea for a story. In your pitch, remember to focus on something that will be interesting to readers. For example, you might suggest a story on how to organize and declutter your home. Do some brainstorming or consider a story based on the most common kinds of questions customers ask you.

While it is not necessary to submit photographs to a daily newspaper editor (most newspapers have their own photographers), photographs may help attract the editor's attention. They might also be published in a smaller magazine, newspaper or newsletter that doesn't have a photographer on staff.

If you send photos (remember to make sure you have permission from the people in the photos as well as the photographer), put them in an attractive two-pocket folder with your business card and a cover letter. Then follow up a week later with a phone call.

Television and Radio Talk Shows

Phone local radio and TV shows to let them know you are available to provide home staging advice to their viewers or listeners. Shows that might be appropriate include morning shows and afternoon talk shows. The person to contact is the producer of each show.

When you contact them, be sure to emphasize how much the show's audience will benefit from an interview with you. Keep in mind that they are not interested in giving you free advertising – their ultimate goal is to improve their ratings, so anyone they interview should be dynamic and interesting.

Also, keep in mind that many station employees are overworked and underpaid. If you can make their job easier you are much more likely to land an interview. The best way to make their job easier is to include a list of "frequently asked questions" with the letter or news release you send them. This is a list of questions that you think listeners might like the answers to. Chances are, whatever you find people asking your advice about are questions that an audience would be interested in, as well.

Write an Article or Column

One of the best ways to establish yourself as an expert is to write articles or a column for a newspaper, magazine, newsletter, or websites. While it can be tough to break into large daily newspapers, there may be an opportunity to write for smaller newspapers or local magazines. Anything you write can be submitted online as well.

You could write on any topic related to home staging (or redecorating), or propose an "Ask the Stager" column where you would answer questions from readers. The length and frequency of your column will depend on the publication. You might produce a weekly 500-word column for a local newspaper, or a monthly 1,000-word column for a newsletter or magazine.

Make sure your article or column provides valuable information to the publication's readers. As with press releases, articles that sound like an ad for your services are not likely to get published. Write about something in your area of expertise; for example, you could write about how to decorate on a budget, or on the latest décor and home decorating trends.

If you are hoping to get published in a newspaper or magazine, phone the editor after you have written your first column or article to ask if they would be interested in seeing it. If so, they will probably ask you to email it. If they want to publish it, they may offer to pay you. However, even if they don't pay, you should consider letting them publish it in return for including a brief bio and your contact information and web address at the end of the article or column.

Online Publicity

As well as offering articles to print publications, consider offering them to online publications. A popular site you can use to distribute your articles is EzineArticles at **www.ezinearticles.com**. Once your articles are posted at EzineArticles, they may be published at a variety of websites and ezines (email newsletters).

You could publish your own blog, using a site such as Blogger (**www.blogger.com**) or WordPress.com (**www.wordpress.com**). However, it can take a while to build up an audience for a blog, and ongoing work to make regular updates. If you don't have time to devote to maintaining your own blog while doing everything else required to build your business, you may be able to get articles you write into other people's blogs by distributing them through EzineArticles.

If you do have a good chunk of time to devote to online marketing, you can also use social networking sites such as FaceBook (**www.facebook.com**) and LinkedIn (**www.linkedin.com**), do micro-blogging (brief updates) at Twitter (**www.twitter.com**), create videos to post at YouTube (**www.youtube.com**), and create pages for sites such as Squidoo (**www.squidoo.com**), among other online marketing activities. Many entrepreneurs find the number of online "social media" sites overwhelming. If you want to learn more about how to use them, consider subscribing to the free Publicity Hound newsletter at **www.publicityhound.com**.

ActiveRain Real Estate Network is a free social network and marketing platform for real estate professionals. This network helps agents to create business relationships both within the industry and with the consumer. Members also include home stagers and other industry groups. Visit their website at **http://activerain.com/action/channels/home_selling/topics/home_staging**.

Even if you decide not to use online social media, you can nevertheless market your business online using methods discussed earlier in this chapter, such as building a website, doing online advertising, and publishing an email newsletter.

5.3.3 Networking

In the home staging industry, networking is an essential ingredient to being a lasting success. Your networking objectives should include finding new prospects, locating referral sources, and meeting other entrepreneurs. The most basic form of networking is word of mouth advertising that is passed from one person to another.

Sandy Dixon of Interior Arrangements believes that "networking is an opportunity to develop mutually supportive business relationships to market yourself and your business with the goal of expanding your prospect base, obtaining more business, and acquiring valuable resources. People network for many reasons—to make friends, get information, identify business prospects, get publicity, stay current professionally—and for those of us who are small business owners, to market our services and products."

While marketing her business, Sandy learned that "a large portion of your revenues will be the direct result of networking efforts, so it is considered a primary means of generating strong repeat and referral-based business."

Every business must work towards building a powerful referral network which delivers revenue. This set of connections should be continuously fine-tuned in order to give you optimum results. Networking is vital for your business because it's inexpensive, it provides a comfortable environment for discussing your services, and it encourages people to promote your business for free.

There are two very distinct groups to target while you are networking. The first group contains the associations you may join to learn more about your industry, usually composed of other professional stagers, redesigners, and decorators. These associations offer potential referral business, opportunities for strategic alliances, and general camaraderie. The second group includes those associations you connect with to meet new people in your community and step out of your comfort zone. These associations will widen your possibilities for finding clients and referral sources.

Network Within Your Industry

You can enhance your visibility and strengthen your business contacts by joining and participating in industry-related groups. List any association call letters next to your name, so that the professional affiliations can be easily seen. Some associations will require the completion of their training course in order to join.

Whatever your reasons for joining a particular industry group, you will probably benefit greatly from the networking, education, and friendships. Simply surrounding yourself with others who share your passions will make you will feel connected to the world.

JoAnne Lenart-Weary, founder of the One Day Decorating Alumni Association, calls this type of relationship "a business buddy" and feels that associations provide that extra push you may need when running a business by yourself. She advises that you "go beyond the…staging industry and join other associations such as the National Association of Professional Organizers or the Interior Design Society."

As part of your industry networking, introduce yourself to others and offer to brainstorm with them on problems they may have. Try to become a friend and ally, even when you don't always get referral business. Find out who lives in your area and determine if they would be interested in joining forces to share advertising expenses.

> **TIP:** The best way to become known in an organization is to be active. Make it your goal to know a lot of people and make sure they know you. Be visible! Networking is an active behavior. Listen to what others have to say, and they will be more open to hearing you out as well.

Refer to section 3.3.3 for links to professional organizations for home stagers.

Network with Your Target Market

While industry networking is important, it's probably even more crucial to connect with your choice clients. For establishing and growing a home staging business, your goal is to network with realtors and property brokers.

As a former real estate agent, Sandy Dixon offers some insider tips for meeting this group and winning them over. She recommends "attending Chamber of Commerce and realtor association events on a regular basis. As they see you becoming a fixture in their arena, you will be taken seriously and be considered a trusted professional."

You should seek out real estate trade shows, rallies, and conventions. Also, enroll yourself in real estate education classes or seminars which are often open to non-realtors. Another tip is to visit the open house events of top agents, but remember to converse with them only when there are no buyers present. If they are busy, check out the property and simply leave your business card or brochure with the agent.

Real estate agents want to know upfront exactly what you can do for them. Sandy offers some helpful hints on how to get face-to-face time with real estate agents. Since she understands how busy they are and what interests them most, she suggests the following ideas:

- "Contact real estate office managers and ask for ten minutes of their time at one of their weekly meetings to introduce yourself and share how your services can benefit both agents and their clients. Offer to sponsor the food for the meeting."
- "Offer the realty office two hours of complimentary staging services prior to an open house in exchange for being invited to participate in the event. Wear a nametag and bring your business cards. Let all those who attend learn about your beneficial services."
- "Suggest that they include a complimentary home staging certificate as part of their listing presentation offering, such as a walk through consultation with a follow-up report or a set number of staging hours."

Your networking objective will be to expand your potential for meeting new people, so that you can tell them what you do for a living. Consumers like to use and refer the services of people they know and trust. Therefore, it's beneficial to join local clubs, women's groups, associations, and other community groups to get your name and face in front of the public. Volunteer your decorating services for their events and special occasions, so your talents are constantly being displayed.

If these groups are not a good fit for you, you might want to try a networking club.

Networking Clubs

Networking clubs typically include one member each from a variety of industries (e.g. insurance, financial planning, law, real estate, etc.). Meetings may include a meal, an opportunity to network, and presentations by speakers. In some clubs, each member is expected to bring a certain number of leads to the group each week or month.

To become a member you are either recommended to the group by an existing member or you might approach the group and ask to sit in as an observer for a couple of meetings then apply for membership if you find the group is a good fit for you. You may be asked to give a short presentation about your own business and what you can bring to the group. The types of activities will vary with different groups, so don't settle on the first one you visit if they don't seem to offer what you're looking for. Make sure the members represent the kind of people you're trying to connect with for clients, or who might know others who would benefit from your services.

One way to find a networking club is through word of mouth. Ask people you know who are in sales such as financial planners. You can also look for networking groups online. Business Network International (**www.bni.com**) has more than 2,300 chapters around the world. Also consider joining a local Meetup group for entrepreneurs. Search for a local group at **www.meetup.com**.

Connecting at a Networking Event

To help you strike up a conversation at a networking event, business consultant Marg Archibald recommends using an elevator pitch and developing a tag line that you can use to quickly identify yourself and what you do. If your tag line is interesting or intriguing people will naturally ask you for more information.

You could try something like:

> *"I'm Lola Stager and I help realtors and homeowners earn thousands of dollars extra each year."*

Once you start talking about your business, ask others about theirs and show an honest interest in what they do; don't start scanning the room for your next prospect. For the next few minutes at least, the person in front of you is the most important person in the room. Meeting people and getting to know them a little better is the first step toward effective networking.

Contractorships

"Contractorships" are business relationships that you form by joining forces with other companies who will create a collaborative and supportive affiliation. Sandy Dixon believes that these networking partnerships will "save your marketing dollars, get you in front of more prospects, and help your partner differentiate themselves from their competition."

You will find contractors in both the retail and service industries. Retail partnerships start with a business that has a physical location and an owner who is willing to team up with you for a special event or to share advertising expenses. Service industry partners are professionals who visit with clients daily to offer services such as realty listings, painting, or home improvements.

In both instances, this is an opportunity to establish a reciprocal referral arrangement whereby you and your contractors have a common interest in serving the same broad base of clients.

Who to Contact

Apart from real estate industry businesses, you'll need to contact and establish relationships with relocation companies, movers, homebuilders, and various home service contractors. These business segments can be very helpful in providing you with leads.

You should also consider contacting these other possible partners: paint stores, florists, wallpaper stores, home accessory stores, gift shops, fashion boutiques, furniture stores, art galleries, wedding consultants, frame shops, event planners, and antique dealers.

Try making a connection with at least one business in each area of expertise, so that you grow a large network of tactical partnerships. A robust group of partners will provide you with ample opportunities to share costs, receive client referrals, and expand your knowledge base.

How to Develop Relationships

So how do you develop strategic relationships with your potential partners? The best way to build up a relationship is by doing business together. First, you have to approach each business owner personally. Ask for an appointment, so that you can introduce yourself and explain how a beneficial relationship would bring about more opportunities for both of you. Referring clients to your company provides great customer service, and it also sets them apart from their competition. They can use your gift certificates or tip books as thank you gifts for their customers, thereby increasing the value of their services.

If the business owner is interested, offer to share an ad in a local publication or split the cost of a booth at an upcoming home show. Many of the larger, corporate retailers will not allow the store manager to make advertising decisions. However, they may have some authority to allow a promotional event or a seminar to bring in customers.

One lucrative idea is to hold an event at a furniture store, home consignment store, or other appropriate retailer. Split the cost of mailing invitations to their client base and running an ad to promote an evening of free decorating tips. You can show a video clip from HGTV and present some quick and easy decorating ideas. Have as many visual aids as possible, and make it fun and casual. Serve refreshments and pass out coupons from both companies. Offer registration for a door prize drawing to obtain a database of potential customers for you and your partner. Be prepared to schedule appointments on the spot.

5.3.4 Promotional Events

Give a Speech or Seminar

Even if you don't join organizations, you may still be able to connect with their members and get new business by being a speaker. Many organizations have speakers for breakfast meetings, luncheons, workshops, and annual conventions.

While you probably will not be paid for your presentations, it can be an excellent opportunity to promote your business. Your company name may be published in the organization's newsletter, it will be mentioned by the person who introduces you, and you will be able to mingle with attendees before and after your presentation. You may get a free breakfast or lunch too!

To let people know that you are available to speak, contact membership organizations mentioned in section 5.3.3 and ask friends and acquaintances if they belong to any groups that have presentations from speakers. To prepare a talk that the audience will find interesting, consider what their needs are. For example, if you're speaking to a local women's group, you could talk about ways to organize and declutter the home, or fun ways to stage a holiday or other party with props and decorations.

Instead of or in addition to speaking for organizations, you could present your own free seminar or workshop. You can hold it at your office, if you have one, or you may be able to rent a meeting room inexpensively at your local Chamber of Commerce or a local hotel or convention center. To help you market your event you could set up a Meetup group at **www.meetup.com**. Although you can ask people to pre-register, you may get some last minute attendees if you accept registrations at the door.

You can also work with your contractors to host free seminars. These presentations usually attract a crowd, so be sure to give the audience valuable information to demonstrate your expertise. Plan on speaking for about 30 minutes and include a question-and-answer session. Let the audience know that you can solve their real estate issues or decorating dilemmas.

To get people to attend, make sure it is a topic that people are interested in, and present it at a time that is convenient for your audience. If you are marketing to corporate clients, schedule your event during business hours. If you are marketing to the public, you're likely to have the best turnout on a Tuesday, Wednesday, or Thursday evening. You're likely to get a larger turnout for a shorter event (e.g. an hour) than one that lasts for hours.

If you give a good talk and offer useful advice, you will be seen as an expert. As long as there are people in the audience who need home staging services, this can be an excellent way to attract clients. On the day that you deliver your speech, be sure you bring plenty of business cards and brochures so you can hand them out to everyone who attends. You'll want people to remember you and have your contact information if they decide they might be able to use your services. You can also show your portfolio or use an easel board with large photographs, and hand out tip sheets or brochures on home staging or decorating.

If you feel your speaking skills could be better, you can get experience and become more comfortable talking to groups by joining Toastmasters, an international organization that helps people develop their speaking skills. To find a Toastmasters chapter near you, you can check your local phone book, call their world headquarters in California at (949) 858-8255, or visit **www.toastmasters.org**.

Another way to engage in public speaking is to teach a course at a local community college. By teaching a continuing education or adult education course, you will publicize your services to the community and earn extra income. If you are considering becoming a staging instructor, this is the best way to acquire teaching experience.

To get started, scan the current classes being offered in the college's course catalog. Contact the person in charge of hiring the continuing education instructors and request an interview. Put together a lesson plan and present it to the department head. Here are some themes that make perfect one-day or multiple-day course topics:

- How to decorate on a budget
- Secret home decorating tips
- Three easy steps to declutter and reorganize your home

- How to choose paint colors and fabrics
- How to perfectly hang wall art

Teach a Class

Teaching a class can be a great way to earn extra money, establish your reputation, and meet prospective clients. You don't have to have a degree to teach adults—just lots of enthusiasm and knowledge of your subject.

The first step is to review the current catalog of continuing education courses offered by local colleges, universities and other organizations that provide adult education classes in your community. Call and ask for a print catalog if they do not have course information at their website. Once you have reviewed their current list of courses, come up with some ideas for new courses. (They already have instructors for any courses that are in their catalog.)

Once you have an idea for a new course in mind, call the college or organization and ask to speak with whoever hires continuing education instructors. They will tell you what you need to do to apply to teach a course.

Trade Shows

A trade show is an event to promote specific types of products and services. If you have ever attended an event such as a "home and garden show", then you have been to a trade show. As a home stager, you may be able to market your services to prospective clients by participating in a show like this.

The cost to become an exhibitor (i.e. to get a booth at the show) will vary depending on the particular show, the location, the number of people expected to attend, and the amount of space you require. It may range from as little as $50 to $1,000 or more for public shows, or up to thousands of dollars for industry shows. To cut costs, you could partner with another non-competing exhibitor and share a booth space.

However, before investing in a trade show booth, attend the event if possible, or speak to some past exhibitors. Find out all the costs involved, what it includes, and what you have to pay extra for (e.g. chairs, carpet, electricity). If the cost to exhibit is too high, you may never recoup the investment and it won't be worth your time and money.

You can find out about upcoming shows by contacting your local convention centers, exhibition halls, or chamber of commerce. You can search for events by industry, type of event and location at **http://directory.tradeshowweek.com/directory/**. For most events, you can then click on a link to find out contact information. Many shows now have their own websites and provide registration information as well as site maps and logistical information.

You'll need to provide your own display. Unless you know that you'll be exhibiting at future shows, look for low-cost options for your display such as getting a local printer to blow up a few photos and signs for your booth. You should also bring business cards, your portfolio and your company brochures for display at your booth, and be prepared to schedule appointments with prospective clients.

One way to attract people to your booth is with a promotional gift such as a list of tips for maximizing the probability of selling a home. When speaking with prospective clients, mention a few of the ideas you have for home staging (but don't give away too much for free). If you don't have an assistant or partner, see if you can find a friend or family member to help out at the show. The days can be long and tiring, and you won't want to close down your booth to take breaks.

6. Success Stories

Now that you're more familiar with the world of home staging, you probably want to meet those who have already prospered in the industry. While you're sure to acquire your own mentors along the way, you'll gain inspiration and expert knowledge by reading about a few people who have already succeeded.

6.1 Meet Debra Gould

Internationally recognized home staging expert Debra Gould is President of Six Elements Inc. and the creator of The Staging Diva® Home Staging Business Training Program. Debra bought, staged, and sold six of her own homes in four cities prior to launching her staging company in the fall of 2002.

Debra is probably the only person teaching the business of home staging who combines an MBA in marketing, almost 20 years experience as an entrepreneur, and the proven track record of growing a successful home staging business herself from scratch—not as a sideline to a real estate practice, but as a stand alone and profitable home-based business.

She knows from first-hand experience what it takes to get a home staging business off the ground with a shoe string budget, and she knows how to attract home staging clients as proven by the hundreds of satisfied clients she's served.

Photo taken by: Virginia McDonald
Debra Gould, The Staging Diva®
President, Six Elements Inc.
www.stagingdiva.com
www.sixelements.com

Debra used her marketing talents to grow her staging company, Six Elements Inc., very quickly, and within the first year she had been featured in prominent magazines like Woman's Day and Reader's Digest, and even appeared on HGTV and Canada's Life Network.

Because of all the requests Debra was receiving from women across the U.S. and Canada, who wanted to start similar businesses, Debra launched the Staging Diva® Home Staging Business Training program in January of 2005. Since that time she has personally trained hundreds of women in the U.S., Canada, Australia, and even South Africa, to start and grow a successful home staging business.

The Staging Diva® program is the only home staging business opportunity recognized by *Entrepreneur* magazine in their Winter 2006 *Be Your Own Boss Guide* and the Summer 2006 *Business Start Ups Guide*.

With 25 years of experience in marketing, Debra delivers an energizing simplicity balanced with a creative sensitivity to everything she does."My mission is to inspire and empower others to live the life of their dreams," says Debra. "Life is too short not to find a way to use our talents and what we enjoy to earn a living. As a mother, I feel it's important to consider what we model for our children. Is it that work is drudgery and something we have to do just to survive, or do we show them that they can actively create their own futures, and do work they love?"

Debra has appeared on *CityTV News* and *GlobalTV News* and has been written about in *The Wall Street Journal, CNNMoney, Fort Wayne Journal Gazette, MoneySense, House and Home, Home & Décor, Style at Home,*

Centre of the City, The Globe & Mail, The National Post, and many other publications. All this exposure generates projects for her Staging Diva® graduates as homeowners and realtors from all over North America contact her looking for home stagers in their markets.

"One of the things I love about staging," says Debra, "is that I can fit clients around the needs of my family. I don't take appointments on evenings or weekends, and I've staged hundreds of houses. Some Staging Diva® graduates only take clients after hours because they have full time jobs and don't want to give them up until their staging businesses are established. Bottom line, you have total flexibility because it's your own company and because of the very nature of the home staging business."

If you're having trouble deciding if the home staging business is right for you, Debra offers a Free Diva Quiz on her website. By requesting the quiz, you can also join a free one-hour group conference call with Debra about the business of home staging where she takes lots of questions from the audience. Quiz takers also get a free monthly subscription to "Staging Diva® Dispatch", filled with home staging business tips and resources to help you start and grow your own staging business.

Debra personally trains all of her students, rather than delegating this to a junior trainer. She brings current real life examples from projects she is staging into every class discussion, so that graduates gain a good understanding of what it's really like to be in the business and how to handle the inevitable challenges that arise. Her program places a priority on the business, marketing, and pricing side of the industry because she feels that even a talented home stager needs this knowledge in order to be a success.

Rather than use the multi-day programs like many competing staging programs, her innovative courses are offered via a live TeleClass format that is just like a telephone conference call. Students are emailed course notes in advance and join Debra at an appointed time by phone over five separate evenings. Some students order recordings of the live TeleClasses and listen at their own convenience.

"If you're considering a home staging career, it's probably because you know you have decorating talent," says The Staging Diva®, "Most students have been decorating for years for friends and family for free, just because they love it. I take that talent they already have and teach students how to turn it into a profitable and creative career."

With a unique mix of creativity, business, and marketing expertise, Debra Gould is an ideal entrepreneur. Whenever she feels the need for encouragement, she evokes one of her much loved quotations by the late economist J.K. Galbraith: "The conventional view serves to protect us from the painful job of thinking."

6.2 Meet Ilyce R. Glink

Ilyce R. Glink
Real Estate and Financial Expert
www.thinkglink.com
www.housetask.com

As an award-winning, nationally-syndicated columnist, television reporter, best-selling author, and radio talk show host, Ilyce R. Glink uses her eclectic background to provide expert advice on everything from real estate to personal finance.

Her syndicated column, "Real Estate Matters", draws a weekly readership of more than four million loyal fans and appears in over 115 newspapers and websites, including the *Los Angeles Times, Detroit Free Press*, and the *Wilmington News Journal*.

As the author of many best-sellers, Ilyce has more than 750,000 books in print including *50 Simple Steps You Can Take To Sell Your Home Faster and For More Money in Any Market*. In this informative book, she covers the entire process of getting a home ready for sale. Her tips describe the home improvements that add the highest value in the shortest timeframe, and she lays out the steps that sellers should take before putting their house on the market. Her valuable real estate guidance continues in her other books, *100 Questions Every Home Seller Should Ask* and *100 Questions Every First-Time Home Buyer Should Ask.*

Ilyce's wealth of knowledge comes from first-hand experience. When asked about the impact of home staging on the real estate industry and the future demand for staging, she shared the following insights:

> "Years ago, the concept of 'home staging' didn't exist. People just cleaned up and polished up their homes. When my husband was selling his first condo, he simply went from room to room, making it look as though it were being photographed for a magazine. He uncluttered spaces, removed many of the books from his shelves, artfully arranged his sculpture pieces, and gave each room a focal point. He sold the condo very soon after it went on the market.
>
> Today, home staging has become a very big business. I recently met a top Realtor in San Francisco who has a very active home staging business outfitting some of the most expensive homes there that are for sale. I toured a $15.5 million home overlooking the bay that had been entirely staged. It was beautiful, right down to the expensive china, silver and crystal used to set the table in the dining room.
>
> The reason staging has become so successful is that home buyers generally lack the ability to imagine how a home will look once their stuff has replaced the seller's. Staging allows a seller to take his own personality out of the home and replace it with one that's more universal.
>
> I do believe home staging will continue to grow, but you have to be careful to find the right person to work with your house. Everyone doesn't have the 'vision' when it comes to staging, just as everyone isn't suited to be a stage designer for the theatre. But if staging helps sell an unsaleable house, or helps a homeowner sell faster and for more money, there will always be a place for it."
>
> —

As a frequent media guest, Ilyce has appeared several times on the *Today Show, Oprah, CBS This Morning,* and Fox News. She can count hundreds of other television and radio appearances on CNN, CNBC, Sound Money, Marketplace Money, and Superstation WGN-TV in Chicago. Additionally, she hosts her own Sunday morning radio talk show, "The Ilyce Glink Show," on Newstalk 750 WSB in Atlanta, Georgia, and also hosts "The Consumer Minute" on a daily basis.

For her diligent efforts, Ilyce has been awarded Best Consumer Reporter and Best Television Report from the National Association of Real Estate Editors. She also won the first Money $mart award from the Federal Reserve Bank of Chicago and received the Peter Lisagor Award for Exemplary Journalism from the Chicago Headline Club.

Ilyce's primary website ThinkGlink.com hosts an abundance of information which is updated on a daily basis. Recently, her company launched several new websites including HouseTask.com, a site with advice and tips for home improvements, remodeling, and repairs.

She offers an online video-on-demand series that covers real estate and financial topics, and she also has a weekly radio show. You can listen to podcasts of the show on her website. Find out more at **www.thinkglink.com/selling**.

6.3 Meet Lori Matzke

Lori Matzke, President
Center Stage Home, Inc.
Minneapolis, Minnesota
www.centerstagehome.com
www.homestagingexpert.com

In the late nineties, after recognizing a need for home staging services in the real estate industry, Lori Matzke founded Center Stage Home. Based in Minneapolis, Minnesota, she started out staging homes and providing pre-sale consultations for both real estate agents and homeowners.

She credits most of her early exposure to an article she wrote entitled "What is Home Staging and How Does it Help Sell My House?" Lori explains how she came to write the article: "In 1999, my business was dying on the vine. It was kind of tough finding clients because no one had a clue what home staging even was." Out of desperation to keep her business afloat, Matzke hastily submitted her article to ABC Real Estate, and they soon added it to their website.

Ten years later, the article still shows up in the "home staging" top 20 list on major search engines and has been reprinted in countless newspapers and trade publications throughout the U.S. and Canada. "Had I known that article would have so much longevity and would do so much to help launch my career, I'd have taken a lot more time and put a lot more thought into writing it," Lori quips.

After introducing her services, it wasn't long before Lori gained enough recognition for her work to attract even more national attention. After numerous inquiries and four years of hands-on experience, she eventually expanded into training and now conducts workshops and seminars nationwide. She began to add affiliates in major cities throughout the U.S., allowing eligible individuals to lease the Center Stage Home name and offering them assistance in marketing their services:

> "Adding training to my list of services was not my original intent but seemed like a natural progression. It has always been my philosophy that the best teachers are those who have 'been there, done that,' and are still working to expand and polish their skills."

In January 2003, Lori was approached by *Realtor® Magazine*, a publication of the National Association of Realtors, and was invited to visit their national headquarters in Chicago to stage two homes for their April 2003 cover story. Since then, she has been featured in numerous print and on-line publications including *CBS MarketWatch, Entrepreneur Magazine*, the *Toronto Star*, the *Chicago Tribune, Decorating Solutions, Divorce Magazine*, and *Parade of Homes*, to name a few.

She has also been showcased on television and radio broadcasts throughout the country including Chicago's ABC Morning News, Fox News in Dallas, KARE 11 and Fox 9 in Minneapolis, and Toronto's Favorite Morning Show. In the spring of 2004, Lori launched Homestagingexpert.com to promote individuals who have earned their HSE, or Home Staging Expert, designation through her course.

Beginning in the fall of 2004, Matzke teamed up with Minneapolis Star Tribune, and real estate staff writer Jim Buchta, to provide full commentary along with before-and-after photos of her work, for the Tribune's bi-weekly feature column, "Staging It." In conjunction with the column, Matzke published her first book in December of that same year, *Home Staging: Creating Buyer Friendly Rooms to Sell Your House*.

When asked about home staging's effect on the real estate industry, Lori says, "In a fast-paced market, a homeowner still wants to sell for the highest possible price. And in a slow market, houses are still selling. Either way, it's always the homes that create a sense of urgency that win over the buyers. Staging your home helps create that sense of urgency. And as any realtor will tell you, the homes that show best, SELL!"

Lori's proficiency in the industry and down-to-earth appeal has allowed her the opportunity to appear as a guest speaker at real estate conventions, home and garden expos, and business conferences across the country. She enjoys sharing her knowledge and experience in the art of staging homes, as well as a relaying her personal account of the perks and perils of starting your own business.

True to her trade, Lori still offers hands-on home staging services and consultations in the Twin Cities Metro area.

6.4 Your Own Success Story

You've proven that you have the interest and drive to launch yourself as an independent home stager. With a little planning and research, and this guide as your handbook, you'll be poised for lasting success in this industry.

Minneapolis-area home staging expert Lori Matzke advises those entering the field to "worry less about your competition and concentrate more on your craft. Realistically, you are never going to be able to stage every home out there. Your style, your personality, and how you relate to potential clients, all play a factor in whether or not someone is going to hire you."

"There are literally thousands and thousands of homes on the market, so there's plenty of business to go around," she says. "Work on fine tuning your own skills and services and getting your name out there, and the business will come....But don't take so much time plotting that your dreams never see the light of day. At some point, you just have to close your eyes and jump!"

Save 50% on Your Next Purchase

Would you like to save money on your next FabJob guide purchase? Please contact us at **www.FabJob.com/feedback.asp** to tell us how this guide has helped prepare you for your dream career. If we publish your comments on our website or in our promotional materials, we will send you a gift certificate for 50% off your next purchase of a FabJob guide.

Get Free Career Advice

Get valuable career advice for free by subscribing to the FabJob newsletter. You'll receive insightful tips on: how to break into the job of your dreams or start the business of your dreams, how to avoid career mistakes, and how to increase your on-the-job success. You'll also receive discounts on FabJob guides, and be the first to know about upcoming titles. Subscribe to the FabJob newsletter at **www.FabJob.com/newsletter.asp**.

Does Someone You Love Deserve a Dream Career?

Giving a FabJob® guide is a fabulous way to show someone you believe in them and support their dreams. Help them break into the career of their dreams with more than 75 career guides to choose from.

Visit www.FabJob.com to order guides today!

More Fabulous Books

Find out how to break into the "fab" job of your dreams with FabJob career guides. Each 2-in-1 set includes a print book and CD-ROM.

Get Paid to Decorate

Imagine having a rewarding high paying job that lets you use your creativity to make homes and businesses beautiful and comfortable. The **FabJob Guide to Become an Interior Decorator** shows how to:

- Teach yourself interior decorating (includes step-by-step decorating instructions)
- Get 10-50% discounts on furniture and materials
- Create an impressive portfolio even if you have no previous paid decorating experience
- Get a job with a retailer, home builder or other interior design industry employer
- Start an interior decorating business, price your services, and find clients

Get Paid to Organize

As a professional organizer you can use your creativity to help people, homes and offices get organized. In the **FabJob Guide to Become a Professional Organizer** you will receive:

- A room-by-room guide to home organizing and reducing clutter
- Valuable information on how to organize businesses including managing workflow, filing systems, and space planning
- Personal organization and time management tips
- Advice to help you start a professional organizing businesses, set your prices, and attract customers

Visit www.FabJob.com to order guides today!